From Here to Financial Happiness

From Here to Financial Happiness

ENRICH YOUR LIFE IN JUST 77 DAYS

Jonathan Clements

WILEY

Published by John Wiley & Sons, Inc., Hoboken, New Jersey.
Published simultaneously in Canada.

Library of Congress Cataloging-in-Publication Data

Names: Clements, Jonathan, author.
Title: From here to financial happiness : enrich your life in just 77 days /
    Jonathan Clements.
Description: Hoboken, New Jersey : John Wiley & Sons, Inc., [2018] |
    Identifiers: LCCN 2018019715 (print) | LCCN 2018020980 (ebook) |
    ISBN 9781119510949 (Adobe PDF) | ISBN 9781119510987 (ePub) |
    ISBN 9781119510963 (hardcover)
Subjects: LCSH: Finance, Personal.
Classification: LCC HG179 (ebook) | LCC HG179 .C65125 2018 (print) |
    DDC 332.024—dc23
LC record available at https://lccn.loc.gov/2018019715

Cover Design: Wiley
Cover Image: © pbombaert/Getty Images

Printed in the United States of America.

F10002773_073018

For June, Joan, and Jerry

Contents

Day One

Start Here,
Go Anywhere

Want to build a happier, more prosperous financial life? All I ask is 5 or 10 minutes a day for the next 77 days. Some days, I'll offer a brief financial lesson. Some days, you'll learn about yourself. And some days, I'll suggest a few simple steps for you to take.

Think of this book as a conversation. It's between you and me – though you should also invite your spouse or partner, if you have one. Have you ever had a conversation where the other people blather on endlessly about themselves while you struggle to get in a single word? It happens all the time, right? I may have written this book, but you'll get to do a fair amount of the talking.

With that in mind, keep a pencil handy. By the time we're done, I hope you'll have scribbled all over this book – and then erased and revised what you earlier wrote. In the coming days and weeks, we'll work to figure out what you want from your financial life, probe your money beliefs, gather information, and take the necessary steps toward a better life.

Along the way, you'll come to understand some of the key ideas needed to be a prudent manager of your own money. Those notions aren't just about dollars and cents. Instead, we'll devote a fair amount of time to the human side of money – why we do what we do and what money can do for us. My fondest hope: By day 77, you'll be thinking of money not as a burden, but rather, as something that's integral to your life and that, with a little effort, can make it so much richer.

> The goal isn't to beat the market, prove how clever we are, or become the wealthiest family in town. Rather, the goal is to have enough to lead the life we want.

Day Two

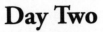

Failure Is Not an Option

We all get just one shot at making the financial journey from here to retirement, and we can't afford to fail. Even if we want to work for the rest of our lives, that simply isn't realistic: One day, our employer or our aging body will force us out of the workforce – and at that point, we'll need a hefty pile of savings.

How can we stack the odds in our favor, so we have a high likelihood of amassing that decent-size nest egg? In the days ahead, we'll focus on some simple, no-nonsense strategies:

❖ Save diligently.

❖ Keep debt to a minimum.

❖ Insure against major financial threats.

❖ Prepare for unemployment.

❖ Hold down investment costs.

❖ Minimize taxes.

❖ Avoid unnecessarily risky investments.

This stuff isn't all that exciting, though the results will be: You'll set yourself on a course that not only brings financial peace of mind today but also ensures a much more prosperous tomorrow.

"But I don't want to be prosperous," you might respond. "I want to be rich."

Depending on how you define rich, that could happen over time, but it won't happen quickly.

"But what if I started day-trading stocks, or borrowed a bunch of money to buy rental properties, or invested in a franchise?"

Yes, those are all potentially faster roads to riches – but they could also be shortcuts to the poorhouse. Never forget that risk and potential reward are inextricably linked. If a strategy holds out the possibility of tremendous wealth, it also runs the risk of terrible failure – and, with the riskiest strategies, terrible failure is the more likely outcome. Our goal: Get you safely and happily from here to retirement.

Life shouldn't be an impulse purchase. We may fall short of our financial plans, but that's better than having no plan at all.

Day Three

Dream a Little

I f money were no object, what would you change about your life? What possessions would you buy? What things would you do? Would you continue with your current job, change careers, or retire? Let your mind wander, conjuring up dreams big and small, and then list them below. These things don't necessarily have to involve money, though there's a good chance that dollars and cents are somehow involved.

I'm not promising you'll be able to turn every wish into reality. But this is your chance to articulate what you want – a crucial first step in figuring out how best to handle your money, while also motivating yourself to make the necessary short-term sacrifices. If we're to say "no" to today's many temptations to spend, we need to make our longer-term goals even more tantalizing.

```
_____
_____
_____
_____
_____
_____
_____
_____
_____
```

In the coming weeks, we'll take the aspirations you have sketched out here and we'll think about them in three broad buckets: daily spending, large purchases, and major life goals. The objective: Fine-tune your list and introduce a dose of reality, so you focus on the dreams that are within reach – and that matter most to you.

> Humans can't sit quietly: We're always fretting, always dissatisfied, always trying to make progress, always trying to divine the future.

Day Four

Embrace Humility

We tend to be a self-confident lot, which is a helpful trait. Those who are self-confident tend to be happier, be more resilient, and enjoy greater career success. But self-confidence isn't nearly so helpful when it comes to managing money. Want to avoid major financial mistakes? We should start by acknowledging five key failings.

First, we don't necessarily know what we want from our lives. We settle on a career and then realize it isn't for us. We buy a house and find it makes our lives harder, not happier. We lust after a luxury car and finally manage to buy it, only to discover it isn't nearly as life-enhancing as we imagined. So what do we want from our lives? It takes a lot of thought, which is why we'll tackle the topic multiple times in the weeks ahead.

Second, we don't know what the future will bring. We imagine tomorrow will look like today. But our lives can be turned upside down in the blink of an eye. We might lose our job, fall seriously ill, meet our future spouse, suffer a death in the family, get divorced, stumble upon the home of our dreams, have a child. Most of us have an astonishing ability to cope with change, and we adapt with surprising speed. As you'll learn in the days that follow, that's both good and bad.

Third, we expect too much from money. Yes, a bigger paycheck and greater wealth can enhance our lives. But blindly pursuing wealth and indiscriminately spending money don't guarantee happiness, and they could backfire. If we devote too many hours to getting ahead in our careers, we'll have less time for friends and family – a crucial contributor to happiness. If we spend without thought, we might accumulate possessions that involve constant upkeep and that prove more of a burden than a blessing.

Fourth, we lack discipline. Given a choice between spending today and saving for tomorrow, we're quick to sacrifice the future. Indeed, many folks seem to engage in magical thinking, imagining that their financial future will be bailed out by high investment returns, a rich aunt's bequest, or the next lottery ticket purchase. But none of these things will likely come to pass. Want to grow wealthy?

For most of us, the road to riches lies in diligently socking away dollars for three or four decades.

Finally, we overestimate our investment prowess. We almost certainly won't pick stocks that beat the market – and it's highly unlikely we'll find someone who can do so on our behalf. We probably won't grow wealthy by flipping homes, trading options, or investing in our sister-in-law's startup. In short, we won't get rich quick, but, with patience and tenacity, we could amass more than enough to live comfortably.

> The meek may not inherit the earth. But they are far more likely to retire in comfort.

Day Five

Twin Wins

Talk to financial advisors and they'll tell you that everybody's financial situation is different, so there are no one-size-fits-all solutions. That's largely true. Still, there are two pieces of advice that apply to everybody – and, if you aren't following them, it's time to start.

First, if you have a 401(k) or similar employer-sponsored retirement savings plan that includes a matching employer contribution, you should sock away at least enough to get the full match. Let's say your employer matches your contributions at 50 cents on the dollar up to 6% of pay. If you contribute 6%, your employer will kick in 3%, for a total of 9%. It's like getting an immediate 50% return on your money. Not contributing the full 6%? Do it today. Failing to contribute enough to get the full 401(k) match ranks as one of the most foolish financial mistakes.

Second, you should never carry a credit card balance – another of the most foolish financial mistakes. Your credit cards might charge 20% interest, and possibly more, on the unpaid balance. Over the long haul, that's far more than you'll likely make by investing your money, even if you invest in the stock market. Got a credit card balance? Make it a priority to get it paid off.

❑ Yes, I'm contributing enough to my employer's retirement plan to get the full match.

❑ Yes, I've paid off all credit card balances or I've got a plan to get it done as quickly as possible.

> You could carry a credit card balance – or you could toss dollar bills out the window. Same thing.

Day Six

Piling It On

Y esterday, I harangued you to fund your 401(k) and pay off your credit cards. Why? Both show the power of *compounding* – for better and worse.

Compounding is the process by which money grows. Each year, we earn returns not only on our original investment but also on gains from previous years that were left in the account.

Let's say our money earns 6% a year. If we invested $1,000 and there was no compounding, we would collect $60 every year, leaving us with $1,600 after 10 years, $2,200 after 20 years, and $2,800 after 30 years. But thanks to compounding, the actual figures are far larger – $1,791 after 10 years, $3,207 after 20 years, and $5,743 after 30 years.

That $5,743 after 30 years is more than twice as large as the $2,800 we would have amassed without compounding. That means roughly half the final account balance came from gains on the original $1,000 investment – but the other half came from investment gains earned on investment gains. We left those gains in the account and they went on to earn additional gains. How cool is that?

Moreover, if we contribute to a 401(k) with an employer match, we'll enjoy compounding both on the money we invest and on the money contributed by our employer. Over time, the results can be spectacular. Let's say we save $5,000 a year for 40 years in a 401(k) plan and our employer matches our contributions at 50 cents on the dollar, so we receive an additional $2,500 each year. Assuming a 6% return, we would have more than $1.2 million after 40 years. What if we put off saving for retirement by just 5 years, so we save and invest for 35 years? Our procrastination would come at a hefty price: We'd retire with 28% less, equal to a $344,000 financial loss.

The combination of credit card debt and time can be just as spectacular – for the credit card company. If we carry a $1,000 balance on a credit card that charges 20% a year, we'll pay $1,488 in interest over the next five years. Think about that: We bought

$1,000 of merchandise, which ended up costing us $2,488. The tab, of course, would climb with every additional year the balance goes unpaid.

> Things that make us feel good today – spending, eating junk food, boozing it up – often leave us feeling worse tomorrow.

Day Seven

Everything's
a Tradeoff

I f we purchase one item, we can't buy something else. If we spend money today, we can't save it for tomorrow. If we decide we want the big house, we'll have less for other goals, like the kids' college and our own retirement.

Our financial lives are a never-ending series of tradeoffs: Every time we use our dollars for one purpose, we relinquish something else. There is, as economists like to say, an *opportunity cost* – and yet we often fail to ponder the opportunities forgone.

How can we get the most out of our dollars? Whenever we open our wallets, we should think not only about what we are getting but also what we're giving up. Unfortunately, this is often a struggle, for two reasons.

First, we get excited about the item right in front of us and make an impulse purchase. Our excitement is so great that it drives out all consideration of possible alternatives. One solution: Hit the pause button. We might impose a 24-hour waiting period, or, if it's a large purchase, maybe a week or two. Even leaving the store for 10 minutes can help us ponder the choice with a clearer head.

But that won't necessarily solve the problem. Why not? There's a second reason we often fail to consider alternative uses for our money: We're hardwired to favor spending today over spending next month or next year.

Economists refer to this as *hyperbolic discounting*. Experiments have found that we'll happily take a small reward today over a far larger reward in a year – even if the larger reward means we would effectively earn a sky-high rate of return over the next 12 months. To keep ourselves on track, we need to be ever-mindful of the impulses that are driving us to spend today and ponder the benefits that can accrue to those who are more thoughtful.

One trick: As we focus on larger future prizes, we should also think about how much we give up if we opt instead for today's imme-diate gratification. We tend to be *loss averse* – meaning we get far more pain from losses than pleasure from gains – so thinking about today's smaller reward as a loss can help keep our worst instincts in check.

Let's say you're 30 years old. Every dollar you spend today might mean giving up $4 of retirement spending – the equivalent of losing three-quarters of your money.

> If we try to keep up with the Joneses, we'll fall ever further behind our unpretentious neighbors with the seven-figure portfolio.

Day Eight

How Happy?

Taken all together, how would you say things were these days? Would you say that you are:

- ❑ Very happy
- ❑ Pretty happy
- ❑ Not too happy

This question has been asked regularly since 1972 as part the General Social Survey. According to the 2016 survey, 30% of Americans say they're very happy, 55% are pretty happy, and 14% are not too happy. These results are remarkably unchanged over the 44 years that the survey has been conducted, even as US average inflation-adjusted, per-capita income has more than doubled.

In other words, we've witnessed a remarkable improvement in our standard of living – more income, improved health care, better cars, larger homes, vastly superior technology – and yet our reported level of happiness hasn't budged. That raises a crucial question: Does money buy happiness – and, if not, why not?

> Why do we save so little? We overestimate the happiness we'll get from spending. But with any luck, repeated disappointments will eventually bring wisdom.

Day Nine

Running the Treadmill

Yesterday, we discussed the General Social Survey. Why hasn't our happiness climbed along with improvements in our standard of living? At issue is a notion known as *hedonic adaptation,* or the *hedonic treadmill.*

We imagine that if we go on a Caribbean cruise, or we buy the bigger house or faster car, or we get a promotion and the accompanying pay raise, we'll be so much happier. And if these things come to pass, we will indeed be happier – but only briefly. Soon enough, the cruise is over and we rarely think about it. All too quickly, we're used to the bigger house, faster car, and larger paycheck, and barely notice these things. Instead, we're onto something else – hankering after another promotion, or a vacation home, or an even faster car.

All this might seem discouraging. But keep two things in mind. First, while we might quickly take the promotion and our latest purchase for granted, there was much pleasure in the pursuit of these goals. We got a lot of satisfaction from working toward the promotion and we were excited as we anticipated the house purchase. The destination may have proven less thrilling than we had hoped, but the journey was great fun.

Second, there are ways to counter hedonic adaptation. We can take a minute to relive the moment when we heard about the promotion. We can pause as we get out of the car and think how lucky we are to own such a fine vehicle. We can look at the photographs from last year's vacation and remember what a blast we had on the cruise.

> Enduring happiness lies in doing meaningful work day after day, week after week, no matter how loud the applause.

Day Ten

What – Me Worry?

A week ago, we talked about your dreams. Today, we'll discuss your worries. Below, write down your top financial concerns:

What would it take to ease these worries? The obvious answer: more money. But the obvious answer might not be the right one. If you ask folks how much they'd need to consider themselves rich, they will often give you a number that's some multiple of their current wealth – whether they are worth $20,000 today or $2 million.

The implication: More money alone may not ease our financial worries. Instead, relief may lie in better understanding what we own, simplifying our finances, keeping closer tabs on what we spend, paying down debt, changing the way we invest, and thinking more about what we need and less about what we want. All this can give us a greater sense of control – a key contributor to happiness.

> If we regularly spend too much, the stuff we buy will never compensate for the stress we feel.

Day Eleven

Lending a Hand

Did yesterday's list of worries include your various debts? Let's see where you stand by filling in five pieces of information below. When adding up your payments on "other debts," include car loans, student loans, and the required minimum payment on your credit cards – though you should always endeavor to pay far more than the required minimum.

- ❏ Your monthly pretax income: $ [   ]
- ❏ Your monthly mortgage payment: $ [   ]
- ❏ Your combined monthly payment for all other debts: $ [   ]
- ❏ Use a calculator to divide your monthly mortgage payment by your monthly income. Multiply the answer by 100 to convert it to a percentage: [   ] %
- ❏ Use a calculator to divide your other monthly debt payments by your monthly income. Multiply the answer by 100 to convert it to a percentage: [   ] %

If you talk to lenders, they'll tell you that you shouldn't be devoting more than 28% of your pretax monthly income to your total monthly mortgage payment, which would include property taxes and homeowner's insurance. What about your other debts? You probably shouldn't be devoting more than 10% of your income to these debts, though it'll be hard to keep below that threshold if you're just out of college and have student loans.

What if you are far above these levels? You have your work cut out for you. Here are six suggestions:

1. Stop using credit cards and put yourself on a cash diet, so you spend no more than the income you have coming in.

2. Focus on paying off the debt with the highest interest rate. That'll usually be credit card debt.

3. If you have loans that are almost paid off – such as student loans or car loans – accelerate payments on these debts, even if the interest rate is relatively low. If you can rid yourself of

these monthly obligations, you'll immediately improve your cash flow.

4. If you have federal student loans, see if you would benefit from one of the income-based repayment programs.

5. If you own a house and have built up some home equity, set up a home-equity line of credit and then use that credit line to pay off higher-cost debt, such as car loans and credit card debt.

6. Investigate refinancing any home, car, and student loans you have. Even if you can't lower the interest rate you pay, you may be able to extend the repayment period, which should lower your monthly payments. The downside: You'll end up paying more interest over the life of the loan.

What if your debts are so large that you see no way out, unless you take more drastic action? To find a reputable nonprofit credit-counseling agency, try the Financial Counseling Association of America (FCAA.org) or the National Foundation for Credit Counseling (NFCC.org).

> If saving money is gratification delayed, borrowing is pain postponed.

Day Twelve

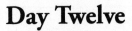

Looking Back

What are the three smartest financial moves you've ever made? These might be specific actions you took or financial habits you adopted.

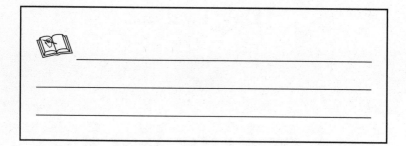

Which three financial actions do you consider your biggest mistakes? These might be things you did – or things you failed to do.

We judge our financial choices by a single, crude yardstick – whether they make us money. But that can result in faulty feedback that validates bad behavior.

Day Thirteen

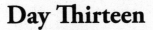

Control What You Can

Take a look at yesterday's list of smart and dumb moves. Now ask yourself: Were your smart moves truly smart – and your dumb moves truly dumb?

For instance, moving a big chunk of money into stocks just before the 2007–2009 market crash might seem like a dumb move. But how could we have known stocks were about to crash? I'd argue that wasn't a dumb move, but rather, bad luck.

The reality is, there's much about our financial lives that we can't control, so luck plays a role. We don't know whether the financial markets will plunge tomorrow. We can't control whether we fall seriously ill and need expensive medical care. We can't stop our employer from shuttering our division and laying off all employees.

Sound bad? While we can't control these things, we can plan for their possibility – by making sure our portfolio isn't too risky, we have health insurance, and our finances can withstand a long bout of unemployment.

Moreover, there's much about our financial lives that we can control and where we have the chance to help or hurt our financial future. Signing up for our employer's 401(k) plan as soon as we're hired is a smart move. Going on a spending spree and maxing out our credit cards is a dumb move. These are both decisions where we're firmly in the driver's seat.

What else can we control? Go back and look at the list of simple, no-nonsense strategies that I offered on day 2. We have a lot of control over how much we save, how much debt we take on, the insurance we purchase, our investment costs, the riskiness of our portfolio, and whether we minimize taxes by making full use of retirement accounts. These are all areas where a little effort can not only pay big dividends, but also help us achieve a greater sense of financial security.

Similarly, we can bring greater calm to our financial lives by sticking with simple investments that we truly understand – a topic we'll tackle tomorrow.

In the short term, many a fool makes money in the markets. But over the long haul, low cost and sensible risk-taking prevails.

Day Fourteen

Keep It Simple

The financial markets are fascinating, overflowing with high-flying stocks, articulate pundits, gee-whiz products, hot fund managers, and the ever-changing drama of each trading day. My advice: Enjoy the show – but if you want to make good money, don't get swept up in the excitement.

The reality is, money management is best when it is simple and cheap. If you don't understand a product, don't buy it. If you don't fully grasp a strategy, don't pursue it. If costs are high, find a less expensive alternative – or skip it entirely. What does that mean in practice? Here are some simple financial products that can be great additions to your family's financial arsenal:

❖ Index mutual funds

❖ Exchange-traded index funds

❖ High-yield savings accounts

❖ Certificates of deposit

❖ Treasury bonds

❖ 401(k) plans

❖ Individual retirement accounts

❖ Health savings accounts

❖ Term life insurance

❖ Rewards credit cards

❖ Conventional mortgages

❖ Home-equity lines of credit

What should you avoid? Below are some products and strategies that are costly or complicated, and sometimes both. Many get heavily pushed by Wall Street – which itself is a warning sign:

❖ Variable annuities

❖ Cash-value life insurance

❖ Equity-indexed annuities

❖ Structured products

❖ Hedge funds

❖ Leveraged exchange-traded index funds

❖ Options trading

❖ Day-trading stocks

❖ Selling stocks short

❖ Market timing

❖ Buying stocks with margin debt

❖ Interest-only mortgages

I was tempted to make the second list even more extensive, adding products that aren't necessarily complicated or costly, but are likely to disappoint. That list would include things like actively managed mutual funds, individual stocks, initial public stock offerings, closed-end funds, and unit investment trusts. The bottom line: If you focus on products on the first list and avoid the products and strategies on the second list, you'll be way ahead of most other investors – and far more likely to succeed financially.

Which products from the "promising" and "perilous" lists do you own? List them below:

Promising	Perilous

In the financial world, complexity may suggest sophistication – but it is usually a ruse to bamboozle and fleece investors.

Day Fifteen

Happy Days

Ass time passes, our memories get airbrushed. We forget the struggles and worries of earlier times and focus on the high points. Yet I wouldn't want to go back and live those days again – and I suspect you wouldn't, either. Perhaps it's because we're a little scornful of our younger, more impetuous selves, and we don't want to be that person again.

But even if you don't want to relive earlier years, you can probably think of a time when you recall being especially happy – and perhaps even happier than today.

- ❑ When was it? (_____)
- ❑ What were you doing? (_____)
- ❑ Who were you with? (_____)
- ❑ How important was money in making this a happy time? (_____)

- ❑ Is there something about this happier time that could guide you today as you ponder how best to use your time and money? (_____)

What's the point of this exercise? It may help you to figure out whether there were things you were passionate about years or even decades ago that you allowed to slip away. Those passions might be the basis for an alternative career, an engaging hobby, or a fulfilling retirement – and they could greatly enhance your life in the years ahead.

> Want to enjoy life more? Put down the remote, back slowly away from the television, and do something where you're a participant, not an observer.

Day Sixteen

Older and Wiser

Research suggests that happiness through life tends to be U-shaped. We start our adult lives reporting a fairly high level of happiness, but our happiness slips through our twenties and thirties, hits bottom in our forties, and then rebounds from there.

What explains this decline and recovery? Nobody knows for sure. One possibility: Early in our adult lives, we tend to be heavily focused on external rewards. We want the promotions and pay raises, as well as the material symbols of success, such as owning a beautiful home and driving a pricey car. And many folks achieve these things, only to discover they don't bring the sense of contentment they expected.

In fact, just the opposite may prove true. We get the promotion, but discover we're more stressed. We buy the home we lusted after, only to find ourselves constantly dealing with maintenance and repairs. Our dissatisfaction often peaks in our forties – the classic midlife crisis.

That is when many folks start to rethink their lives. Maybe striving for promotions isn't the road to happiness. Instead, maybe what matters is doing work we love. Perhaps more possessions won't make us happier. Instead, perhaps we should spend our money on experiences, especially experiences enjoyed with family and friends, because those occasions seem to deliver a big boost to happiness.

The upshot: As we age, we become less interested in earning the approval of others, whether by getting ahead at work or by flaunting status symbols – and more focused on doing things that are important to us.

> Spend on experiences or possessions? Experiences deliver fond memories. Possessions deliver repair bills.

Day Seventeen

Life Support

W hat's the minimum amount of money you need each month to keep your financial life afloat? We're talking here about fixed costs – expenses that come around with regularity and are tough to cut, at least in the short term. Put dollar amounts next to the items below. To make sure you don't miss anything, spend some time leafing through your checkbook and looking at old credit card statements. If your mortgage payment includes property taxes and homeowner's insurance, there's no need to break out these figures separately.

Mortgage or rent	
Property taxes	
Home maintenance	
Car payments	
Other car costs (gas, servicing)	
Utilities	
Cable	
Phone	
Internet	
Groceries	
Insurance premiums	
Other	
TOTAL	

Financial freedom isn't the ability to buy anything we want. Rather, it's knowing we already have what we need.

Day Eighteen

Desperately Seeking Solvency

F inancial experts constantly exhort us to have an emergency fund. They typically recommend keeping three to six months of living expenses in so-called cash investments – savings accounts, money market funds, and similar ultra-safe investments.

Why keep so much cash? The fact that this is expressed as "months of living expenses" is the giveaway. This isn't about emergencies like repairing the car or replacing the refrigerator. You could probably tackle those expenses fairly easily. Instead, an emergency fund is really an unemployment fund. Losing your job is the big financial emergency.

Yesterday, you put a number on your monthly fixed living costs. Now, imagine you were out of work and needed to live off savings, unemployment benefits, and other sources of spending money. Where would you turn to cover your fixed monthly costs?

If you tapped the resources you've listed, how long could you cover expenses before your financial life started unraveling? Estimate the number of months:

As you consider how much emergency money you need access to, give some thought to how long it might take to find work. Much depends on the position you would be hunting for. If you lost a job waiting tables at a restaurant, you could probably find something similar within a week. But if you're a senior executive, it might be a year or more before you found anything comparable.

> Want to reduce financial stress? All it might take are less debt, a few thousand in the bank and a regular savings program.

Day Nineteen

Sleeping Better

When folks are out of work, they often do a heap of damage to their financial future. They rack up huge amounts of credit card debt. They take desperate measures, like skipping mortgage payments and defaulting on auto loans. They cash in retirement accounts, triggering income taxes and tax penalties – and putting their retirement at risk.

Would you have to take such steps? Go back and look at what you wrote yesterday. If you don't currently have the financial where-withal to deal with a prolonged period of unemployment, consider four steps:

1. Figure out which expenses you would immediately slash if you lost your job – and ponder whether you ought to cut some of those expenses today. The lower your living costs, the longer your savings would last.

2. Decide how many months of living expenses you want saved as an emergency fund and what that means in total dollars. Next, open either a high-yield savings account or a money market mutual fund. A quick internet search will help you identify high-yield savings accounts. Meanwhile, Vanguard Group regularly has some of the highest-yielding money market mutual funds, thanks to the firm's legendary low investment expenses. Once you have an account set up for your emergency money, arrange to contribute automatically every month until you hit your target amount.

3. If you own a house, set up a home-equity line of credit. It'll be a paperwork hassle to establish the credit line and you might have to pay an annual fee of $50 or so. But in return, you'll have easy access to borrowed money. Ideally, you would never use the credit line – but it's best to be prepared.

4. Fund Roth individual retirement accounts. You can withdraw your regular annual contributions to a Roth IRA at any time for any reason, with no taxes and penalties owed – flexibility you get with no other retirement account, including a Roth 401(k). It's only if you touch a Roth IRA's investment

earnings that taxes become an issue. Ideally, as with a home-equity line of credit, you'd never tap your Roth IRA for emergency money, and instead leave the account to continue growing tax-free.

These steps won't just help if you find yourself out of work. They'll likely also give you a greater sense of financial security – and, fingers crossed, you will find yourself worrying less about money.

❑ Yes, I have a high-yield savings account or money market fund, and it either holds enough to cover a period of unemployment or I'm adding automatically to it every month.

> If we want to feel better about our finances today, we should spend more time thinking about how we'll pay for tomorrow.

Day Twenty

Home Schooling

What did you learn about money from your parents? These lessons might have been things they tried to teach you or things you learned by observing their behavior and listening to their conversations. Use the space below to write down the childhood lessons that come to mind. They might relate to spending, borrowing, saving, investing, insurance, cars, real estate, or perhaps some other money-related topic.

Look at what you just wrote. Which of these beliefs do you now call your own, and which have you cast aside?

Kept	Discarded

Our children are more likely to follow our financial example than our financial advice.

Day Twenty One

True Believers

We all have strong ideas about money, sometimes without realizing it. We often don't appreciate how ingrained our beliefs are until we end up in a relationship – and our spouse or partner insists there's a better way.

Yesterday, we probed what you learned about money from your parents and whether you made those ideas your own. You might have picked up additional ideas from friends, colleagues, experts, advertising, television shows, and movies. To figure out what beliefs you've adopted, jot down answers to the eight questions below. If you are in a long-term relationship, you might also pose these questions to your spouse or partner.

1. Is it important to drive a nice car?
2. Should getting as rich as possible be one of your overriding life goals?
3. Is a home a good investment?
4. When is it okay to go into debt?
5. Is the stock market a good place to invest, or far too dangerous?
6. Should investors try to beat the market?
7. How much financial help should you give a child?
8. If you have the money, should you pay off your mortgage early?

In the weeks ahead, we'll touch on all eight topics. With any luck, you'll find yourself thinking harder about your money beliefs – and perhaps even revising some of them.

> What matters is what you focus on. Want to be happier? Don't focus on the wealth of others or the possessions you don't have.

Day Twenty Two

Hunting but Not Gathering

Each of us is a bundle of hardwired instincts – and yet often we're only dimly aware of what these instincts are. That, of course, is the nature of instincts: They're things we do without stopping to think.

Most of the time, our instincts are a huge help. They tell us to pull our hand away from the hot pan, before we get scorched, and help us to figure out who's the friendly stranger on the crowded street who will give us directions. These are the instincts that were honed by our hunter-gatherer ancestors and which allowed them to survive and reproduce. Be impressed: Without them, none of us would be here today.

But while our nomadic instincts steer us mostly in the right direction, they can lead us astray in the modern financial world:

- ❖ We're inclined to consume whenever we can, and we quickly become dissatisfied with what we have. Eating whenever possible, and constantly striving for more, made sense for our ancestors. But today, these instincts can cause us not only to overeat but also to overspend and take on too much debt.

- ❖ We believe the key to success is working hard. It's an attribute that helped our ancestors survive and also helps us get ahead in today's work world. But our belief in hard work, coupled with our self-confidence, can cause us to incur hefty investment costs and take too much risk, as we trade excessively, hunt for elusive stock market winners, and make big investment bets.

- ❖ We imitate others. That was how our ancestors learned to hunt, fish, and build shelters. Today, however, imitating others can lead us to buy popular, overpriced investments.

- ❖ We're hardwired to detect patterns. For our ancestors, that was a helpful skill, as they hunted animals and anticipated changes in the seasons. But today, our search for patterns can deceive us into believing we know what will happen next in the financial markets, when all we're really seeing are random price movements.

❖ We hate losing. That was an understandable instinct for our nomadic ancestors, because losing food or shelter could mean death. Today, however, our loss aversion causes us to shy away from stocks, which may suffer nasty short-term losses – but have the potential to deliver healthy long-run gains.

❖ We're heavily focused on the here and now, and we put a low value on the future. For our ancestors, that made sense: They didn't have to worry about saving for retirement. The problem is, today, those instincts can cause us to save too little and ignore our long-term goals.

How can we overcome these instincts and keep ourselves on the right financial track? Often, the key is to hit the pause button and allow the contemplative side of our brain to wrestle with the instinctive side. Tempted to make a major purchase or a big change to your portfolio? If you want to avoid a decision you'll later regret, try mulling it over for a few days.

> *Homo economicus* may always behave rationally. But the rest of us try not to keep too much chocolate in the house.

Day Twenty Three

Fixing to Win

Grab your latest paystub. You'll probably also need recent bank and credit card statements. Start with monthly pretax income – and figure out how it gets divvied up among these four categories:

Fixed living costs	
Discretionary expenses	
Taxes	
Savings	
TOTAL	

Fixed costs include your rent or mortgage, car payments, insurance premiums, property taxes, utilities, internet, phone, groceries, and other regularly recurring expenses. If you recall, you calculated this number back on day 17.

For taxes, you'll want to include federal and state income taxes, as well as Social Security and Medicare payroll taxes. If you're an employee, this information should be on your paystub. For savings, include any contribution you make to your employer's retirement plan, which should also be on your paystub. To that amount, add any other money you sock away each month.

Take your pretax income and subtract your fixed living costs, monthly savings, and taxes. Result? Whatever is left should be your discretionary expenses – spending on fun stuff like eating out, concerts, hobbies, and vacations.

Is your financial life in balance? Focus on two numbers. Ideally, your fixed living costs should be eating up no more than 50% of your income. Meanwhile, unless you'll receive a traditional employer pension, you ought to be socking away at least 12% of your income toward retirement. Your total savings rate should be even higher if you have other goals, like building up your emergency fund or putting aside dollars for the kids' college.

Not saving enough? Don't spend much on discretionary "fun" expenses? In all likelihood, the problem is that your fixed living costs are too high. You might be able to cut them here and there by raising the deductibles on your insurance policies, opting for a smaller cable package, and spending more carefully at the grocery store. But for most Americans, their two biggest expenses are their home and their car. If your fixed costs are well above 50% of income, you may need to take drastic steps to bring down those two expenses.

❑ Yes, my fixed living costs are at or below 50% of my pretax income.

❑ Yes, I am saving at least 12% of my pretax income toward retirement.

❑ Yes, I am also socking away additional money for my other goals.

> No matter how good the sale, you always walk out the store with less money.

Day Twenty Four

What It Takes

Think about three friends or family members who you know are comfortable financially. A warning: Stick with folks you're highly confident are in good financial shape – and don't rely on outward appearances alone. List the three people here:

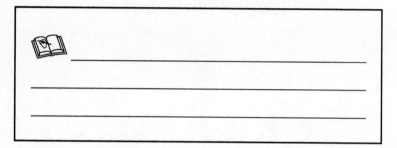

What have been the keys to their financial success? List the attributes below. Each attribute won't necessarily apply to all three people.

If our goal is to have more money than others, we'll never have enough.

Day Twenty Five

Be Kind to Your Future Self

The secret to financial success is no secret at all: We need great savings habits. Yes, we can bolster our wealth by investing wisely and hurt it with foolishness. But without great savings habits, investment prowess – or lack thereof – is immaterial. After all, if we have just $1,000 invested, it doesn't much matter whether we earn 2% over the next year or 20%. In dollar terms, that would mean $20 in gains or $200 – hardly the stuff of which comfortable retirements are made.

Look at the folks you listed yesterday and the characteristics that made them successful. They may have earned handsome salaries, invested astutely or built their own business. But the reason any of those financial advantages turned into significant wealth was because they were good savers.

Consider adopting these folks as your role models. You might ask them about their success and use their stories to motivate you. You might even tell them about your financial goals. That could further motivate you, as you strive to look good in their eyes.

Indeed, financial success is as much about mindset as anything else. To be a good saver, we obviously need an income – and the higher that income, the easier it'll be to save. But there are five other attributes we also need:

❖ *Low fixed costs.* Why do many families fail to save? As I alluded to on day 23, often they simply can't, because they have boxed themselves in with a litany of monthly fixed costs, everything from mortgage payments to insurance premiums to recurring fees for phone, internet, cable, music streaming, and more. Result: They have so little financial wiggle room that it's almost impossible to save.

❖ *Self-control.* Even with low fixed costs, saving can be a struggle because temptation abounds. When something catches our eye, we need to squash the impulse to immediately open our wallet. By delaying gratification, we'll have time to consider whether it's truly money well-spent. For some, this is easy. For many, it's hard – in the same way it's hard to eat less and exercise more.

❖ *An aversion to financial stress.* Spending may give us a short-term thrill. But excessive spending can also lead to ongoing financial stress, as we discover we can't pay the credit card bill and maybe not even the rent. As we come to appreciate how terrible that stress can be and how great it feels to have our finances under control, spending can lose its allure.

❖ *Self-reflection.* When we're young, it isn't surprising that we spend too much on items that deliver little happiness. We simply haven't had time to learn from experience. But as the spending disappointments pile up, we gradually come to appreciate how little happiness we receive from our purchases. Self-control is no longer a problem, because the goodies no longer seem tantalizing. The sooner we get to this point, the easier it'll be to lasso our spending and get on the right financial track.

❖ *A fondness for our future self.* If we spend money today, we can't spend it tomorrow, let alone in 30 years. If we're rational, we would care more about the future when we're younger, because there's potentially so many years ahead of us. But ironically, it seems our concern for our future self grows as we get older.

> What's the common attribute of everyday Americans who have amassed $1 million or more? They're extremely frugal – otherwise known as cheap.

Day Twenty Six

Ups and Downs

Give some thought to a typical week. Which moments do you enjoy the most? Which activities do you find most absorbing? Make a list:

_____

_____

_____

_____

_____

_____

_____

_____

_____

_____

_____

_____

Again, think about a typical week. Which parts do you dislike the most?

_____

_____

_____

_____

_____

_____

_____

_____

_____

_____

_____

_____

_____

_____

It isn't the bigger house, the new furniture or the remodeled kitchen that'll make you happy. It's the people you live with.

Day Twenty Seven

Enjoying Your Dollars

Look at yesterday's list of your week's happiest and least happy moments. Could you find a way to have more of the happy moments – and less time devoured by activities you don't enjoy?

As you mull that question, think about money from two different angles. First, what role does it play? At first blush, the connection might appear tenuous. If you love coaching your kid's soccer team and hate commuting, money might seem like an incidental consideration. But changing your life – so you worked at home more or spent less time commuting, thus giving you more time with your child – might involve getting a new job or moving closer to the office.

Second, could you change the way you spend, so you increase the good times and devote fewer hours to things you don't like? For instance, you might budget more for restaurants if you love eating out, while also hiring a landscaping service if you loathe yardwork.

Got ideas for how to make your weeks more enjoyable? List them here:

Sometimes, we don't use money to make ourselves happy. Rather, we use it to fend off unhappiness. Almost all of us have an Achilles' heel – a weakness that causes us shame. We might even keep it a secret from others. It might be gambling, spending excessively, drinking, taking drugs or overeating.

Give some thought to your weakness or weaknesses. Are they acceptable human failings, or should you seek to change? What's the financial impact of your weaknesses – and are they affecting your ability to achieve your financial goals? Suppose you gave into your weaknesses not just today, but every day for the next 12 months. How great would the cumulative damage be – and is the thought sufficiently scary to motivate you to change?

To summon the willpower needed to keep our worst instincts at bay, often we need to take better care of our physical selves by spending time outside, sleeping longer, and exercising. When we fail to do these things, our ability to ward off temptation is weakened – and we can find ourselves eating, drinking, and spending more, as we seek a short-term boost to our spirits.

> Money may feel like our scarcest resource, especially when we're younger. But in truth, our most finite resource is time.

I f you just graduated college, you might have an alarming amount of student loans and perhaps also credit card debt. Yet, arguably, you are rich, because ahead of you lies four decades of paychecks. According to the Census Bureau, the estimated lifetime earnings of a college graduate average $2.4 million, figured in today's dollars. Economists refer to this income-earning ability as our *human capital,* and it has four key implications for how we manage our money:

- ❖ *We can borrow against it.* Taking on debt early in adult life – especially to pay for college and to buy a home – can make financial sense. The money borrowed allows us to buy items we can't currently afford, plus we know we have many income-earning years to service these loans and get them paid off by retirement. But we should be careful not to overdo it: We don't want to borrow more than we can comfortably repay, and we should be careful to use debt to advance our financial lives, not pay for extravagances we'll likely later regret.

- ❖ *We need to protect our human capital.* In case we can't work because of injury or illness, we should have disability insurance. If we have a family that depends on our paycheck, we probably also need life insurance. What if we lose our job? That's the chief reason to sock away some emergency money.

- ❖ *Our human capital provides the dollars we need to set aside for retirement.* In essence, our working years are about taking the income kicked off by our human capital and turning it into a large pile of financial capital, so one day we can retire – and live without the income from our human capital.

- ❖ *Our paycheck frees us up to invest in stocks.* Because our human capital provides us with income, there's less need to buy conservative, income-generating investments. Instead, we can gun for long-run growth by investing in the stock market.

> For most of us, our most valuable asset is our income-earning ability. We shouldn't double-down on that bet by buying our employer's stock.

Day Twenty Eight

The Human Touch

Day Twenty Nine

Taking Charge

Who depends on you financially? For some, the answer is nobody. If we never again earned another paycheck, it might be a problem for us. But for those we know and love, there would be no financial ill effect.

For others, there are many dependents. If we stopped earning an income, it might have financial repercussions for our spouse or partner, our children, and perhaps others. Below, list those who depend on you financially.

Give some thought as to how long you'll need to provide financial support. If you have a spouse who doesn't work, you would likely be looking to cover all household expenses for the rest of your – and his or her – life. For your children, that financial support might end with high school or college. All this should factor into both your college savings strategy, which we will address on day 53, and your estate plan, which we'll tackle starting on day 70. But it also has implications for your insurance coverage – and that's where we'll turn tomorrow.

Who	How Long

Don't have a will? You won't live to regret it, but your family almost certainly will.

Day Thirty

Everybody in the Pool

What is insurance? Forget all the fine print – the deductibles, the special riders, the exclusions, the nitpicky legal language. At its heart, insurance is about *pooling risk*. You, me, and a bunch of other folks contribute to a pool of money overseen by an insurance company. Those who suffer misfortune receive money from the pool. The rest of us pay our premiums and get nothing in return, which is what we want, because it's a sign that life is good.

Insurance can be used to protect ourselves financially against all kinds of misfortune, including our house burning down, getting sick, crashing the car, suffering a disability, getting sued, and dying and leaving our family destitute.

Depending on our situation, some of these risks will loom larger than others. For instance, if we're age 40 and die suddenly, it could be a major problem for those who depend on us financially, and carrying some life insurance would likely be a good idea. But if we're a 70-year-old retiree, it's far less of a financial problem. At that point, any kids would likely have left home. What if we have a spouse? He or she might be sad about our death but, if anything, would likely be in better financial shape. After all, the nest egg intended for two now has to pay for just one retirement. The implication: Life insurance almost certainly isn't needed.

Because insurance will – we hope – be a money loser, we want to purchase only the policies that are absolutely necessary. Think about all the financial risks you face. If you can handle these risks on your own, no insurance is needed. If the financial fallout would be too great for you and your family to shoulder, you probably need insurance. My advice: Buy all the insurance policies you need, with as little coverage as you can get away with.

> We should view ourselves not as pursuers of performance but as managers of risk.

Day Thirty One

Cover Me

On days 18 and 19, we discussed how you would cope if you were out of work for perhaps six months. But what if you never worked again because you suffered a career-ending disability – or an untimely demise?

If you're single with no dependents, death isn't a financial problem, because nobody would be left in the lurch. Thus, there's no need for life insurance. A disability, on the other hand, could be a huge problem. How would you support yourself if you were physically unable to work and couldn't pull in a paycheck? If you do indeed have a family, how would you support them?

Social Security may pay benefits if you're disabled, but qualifying is difficult: You need a disability that's so severe that it will prevent you from working for at least 12 months or it'll result in death. Even if you are deemed eligible, it can take more than five months for benefits to begin.

With Social Security disability benefits difficult to obtain, many employers provide short-term and long-term disability coverage. What if your employer doesn't? What if you work for yourself? Seriously consider purchasing disability insurance. That might seem unnecessary, especially if you have a desk job where you're unlikely to get injured. Keep in mind, however, that most disabilities result not from accidents but from illness.

If you have a family who depends on you financially, you might also need life insurance. Your best bet will likely be a low-cost term insurance policy, rather than the super-expensive cash-value policies that insurance salespeople love to sell. How much coverage should you get? You might buy a policy with a death benefit big enough to pay off the mortgage and any other debt, fund college accounts for the kids, and cover the family's living costs for maybe three to five years, as they adapt to living without you and your paycheck.

If you already have significant savings, you could likely make do with a policy that has a somewhat smaller death benefit. A rule of thumb: If you have $1 million in savings and investment accounts, you can probably skip not only life insurance but also disability coverage as well.

❑ Yes, I have either disability insurance or enough savings to cover my lifetime living costs.

❑ Yes, I have a family that depends on me, but I have enough term life insurance and savings to ensure they'd be okay financially.

You could update the beneficiaries on your life insurance and retirement accounts – or you could keep things simple and leave everything to your ex-spouse.

Day Thirty Two

Just in Case

Here's a horrifying thought: You could potentially need up to eight different types of insurance. Here are the eight policies:

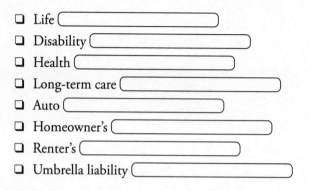

- ❑ Life
- ❑ Disability
- ❑ Health
- ❑ Long-term care
- ❑ Auto
- ❑ Homeowner's
- ❑ Renter's
- ❑ Umbrella liability

Sound like a family budget buster? The good news is, very few people will need all eight policies – and there are ways to trim the cost of the insurance you do need. For instance, if you own a home, you should have homeowner's insurance and, indeed, your mortgage company will require it. But you might get a policy with, say, a $5,000 deductible. True, that means the first $5,000 of loss will come out of your pocket and you need to be prepared for that financial hit. But thanks to that high deductible, your premiums will be significantly lower, and yet you'll still be protected against the big financial hit triggered by, say, your home burning down.

The same philosophy should apply to the deductibles on your health and auto insurance, and also to the elimination period on your disability and any long-term-care insurance. A long elimination period is like a high deductible – but, in this case, it's the time between when you make your claim and when benefits start getting paid.

As you grow wealthier, you may be able to drop policies. As I mentioned yesterday, if you have $1 million or more in savings, there's probably no need to have life and disability coverage, and you could likely also skip long-term-care insurance. Even if you haven't yet hit $1 million, you might scale back coverage as your net worth increases.

While rising wealth might prompt you to cut back on other insurance coverage, it should make you more anxious to get umbrella-liability insurance. Why? Your growing wealth may make you a more attractive target for the litigious. If you're sued, an umbrella policy can provide protection – and the price of this protection is a relatively modest annual premium.

Next to the list of policies above, put a check mark against those you have or ought to get. Also note any changes you plan to make, such as reducing coverage or increasing deductibles.

> Sunshine is the best disinfectant: Schedule a time to show your financial statements to a friend, and you'll rush to clean up your finances.

Day Thirty Three

Hits and Misses

Recall the significant expenditures you've made during your adult life – things like buying homes, purchasing cars, paying for college, vacations, home remodeling projects, footing the bill for a wedding, enduring hobbies, and major furniture purchases.

Which three are most likely to make you smile?

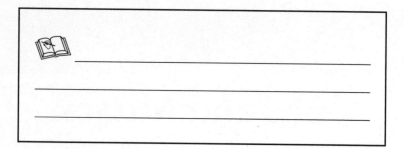

Which three expenditures disappointed you – and perhaps even triggered pangs of regret?

Start life in first class, and you'll take it for granted. Occasionally get upgraded, and it'll be a real treat.

Day Thirty Four

Wishes Come True (Maybe)

A week ago, we thought about your everyday spending and pondered how you might use your dollars differently so you can squeeze more happiness out of your money. Today, we'll think about bigger purchases – maybe much bigger.

It's time to create a wish list of expenditures you might make over the next few years. There are all kinds of possible choices: a new car, new living room furniture, a major remodeling project, a special vacation, or extravagant weddings for your adult children. As you draw up the list, glance back at what you wrote yesterday and ponder the major purchases that brought you happiness in the past, as well as those that failed to do so.

In creating your wish list, there are two goals. First, it's a chance to have a little fun. Who doesn't like to daydream? Second, by drawing up a list, you can compare different possibilities and consider which should be a priority and which aren't such a great idea. My advice: Revisit the list every month or two. Some items will quickly slip off the list, but others will stay – an indication that these could be worthy uses for your hard-earned dollars.

_____

_____

_____

_____

_____

_____

_____

_____

_____

_____

Basements are badly curated museums dedicated to the purchases we regret but can't yet bring ourselves to trash.

Day Thirty Five

Peering Forward, Glancing Back

Wh*hen we remodel the kitchen or take an expensive vacation, we imagine the great pleasure that will come when the kitchen is finally finished or when we're actually on the trip. And while those may prove to be high points, the potential for increased happiness extends far longer.

In fact, we may discover that the best time is the period before, when we're contemplating the new kitchen and planning the vacation. At that juncture, we can daydream, conjuring up all kinds of possible kitchens and visualizing trips to a host of exotic locations. And after we settle on our plans, we can eagerly anticipate the new kitchen and the upcoming trip, musing about how great things will be.

But once the kitchen is done and the trip is over, it's easy for both to slip from our minds. We adapt to the new kitchen and take it for granted. We forget about the trip. What to do? To squeeze a little more happiness from the dollars we spent, we should pause occasionally, admire the new kitchen, and think how lucky we are. We should look at the photos from the trip and recall the good time that we had.

While both the kitchen and the trip can be sources of ongoing happiness, we will likely find that the trip scores better on that front. That might seem counterintuitive. After all, the kitchen is still there, present in our lives. But that's also the problem. As with other possessions, we'll have to watch the kitchen age over time. The cabinets will get scuffed up, the plumbing will need to be repaired and the appliances will have to be replaced.

By contrast, the trip – like other experiences – won't deteriorate over time. Quite the contrary: We may remember the vacation ever more fondly, as we forget the incidental annoyances and focus on the highlights. This is another reason experiences tend to deliver more happiness than possessions.

> If we fancy something today, we should buy it tomorrow. That'll give us time to savor the purchase – and ponder whether it's money well spent.

Day Thirty Six

Driving Yourself Crazy

According to the Bureau of Labor Statistics, 33% of the average American family's spending gets lavished on housing, including mortgage or rent, property taxes, utilities, and furniture. Another 16% goes toward transportation, with a big chunk eaten up by our cars, whether it's buying or leasing them, filling them with gas, or paying for insurance.

Add it up, and almost half of our spending is devoted to our homes and our cars. We all need somewhere to live and a way to get around town. But are you spending too much on housing and transportation? Let's take a look at your car or cars.

How much are you spending? Estimate your total annual car costs:

Car payments	
Gas	
Insurance	
Regular servicing	
Registration	
Other	
TOTAL	

Now, ask yourself: Does your total expenditure on your car or cars seem reasonable relative to your annual income – or are you spending too much?

Whenever you see a pricey car roll down the street, hold a moment of silence to mourn the wealth departed.

Day Thirty Seven

Wheeling Dealing

Spending isn't bad. What's bad is spending too much – or spending on items we don't much care about. For some folks, cars are a passion, so spending a hefty chunk of their income on their family's vehicles might be a good use of their money. That'll leave them with less money for everything else, but the tradeoff could be worth it.

What if cars aren't your passion? In that case, you should focus on buying the sort of vehicle that makes sense for your family at a reasonable cost. This is not especially complicated. There are two basic rules if you are buying a car for its utility, rather than because you want to impress the neighbors or have the pleasure of driving a car that's somehow distinctive.

First, think twice before buying a new car, because you'll pay a premium price. Much of a car's depreciation occurs in the first three or four years – plus, a new car is costlier to replace and hence costlier to insure.

Second, the more often you change vehicles, the more you'll incur in costs, thanks to sales taxes, car registration fees, and markups charged by dealers.

The upshot: Your best bet is probably a three-year-old car with 20,000 to 30,000 miles on it, so much of the depreciation has already occurred, but there are still plenty of miles left to drive before it becomes unreliable. Thanks to all the three-year-old cars that come off lease each year, you should have plenty of choice. You might then aim to drive the car for at least six or seven years.

> "The lease payments could hurt your ability to fund your 401(k)," said no car salesman ever.

Day Thirty Eight

Taking Credit

A lofty credit score has become one of America's most coveted status symbols, which is a little sad, because it's all about borrowing money. Your credit scores are based on your credit reports, which are largely a recitation of the money you've borrowed over the years, whether through mortgages, auto loans, or credit cards.

The three major credit bureaus, Equifax, Experian, and Trans-Union, take that information and convert it to a numerical score. The most popular scoring system is the FICO score, which ranges from 300 to 850. An average score is around 700 and a score of 750 or above indicates you're considered a very good risk.

You should check your credit reports periodically and especially before applying for a car loan, mortgage, or other large loan. Look for incorrect information, such as payments that are shown as late when they weren't, and check for debts that are listed more than once. Also check for accounts you don't recognize. That could be a sign you're a victim of identity theft.

If you are about to apply for a mortgage or car loan, you should also check your credit score. That might cost you a small fee, though scores are increasingly available at no charge through credit card referral websites (think Credit Karma, WalletHub, and their ilk) and from a variety of financial firms, including Capital One, Chase, and Discover.

Credit scores aren't just viewed by lenders. They're also used by insurance companies when setting premiums and by landlords when vetting tenants. Meanwhile, potential employers can view a version of your credit report, but not your credit score.

Unfortunately, identity theft has become a growing problem. How can you protect yourself? In addition to checking your credit reports regularly, consider three strategies. First, you might freeze your credit with the three major credit bureaus, which should prevent someone from applying for credit in your name. This will provide the greatest protection – but it's a hassle if you are still regularly applying for new loans and credit cards, because you'll need to unfreeze your credit each time.

As an alternative, you might opt for the second strategy: Place a fraud alert on your credit file at the three credit bureaus. That way, lenders have to take extra steps to confirm your identity before opening an account in your name.

What's the third strategy? You could sign up for credit monitoring, which is available free from a host of websites (again, think Credit Karma, WalletHub and their ilk). Credit monitoring is the least satisfactory solution. By the time you're alerted that somebody has applied for credit in your name, you already have a problem – but it should allow you to move swiftly to stop the theft.

- ❑ Yes, I've been to AnnualCreditReport.com to get free copies of my credit reports.
- ❑ Yes, I'm about to apply for a loan, so I've checked my credit score to see where I stand.
- ❑ Yes, I have frozen my credit, placed a fraud alert, or signed up for credit monitoring.

> Debt allows us to buy items we can't currently afford. This is known either as "consumption smoothing" or "sticking a finger in your own eye."

Day Thirty Nine

Running Up
the Score

Because credit scores are so important, you want to nurture the highest score possible. Some of the steps involved aren't obvious, but most are – and they're the sort of thing you ought to be doing as a prudent manager of your own money. Here are six strategies that can help your credit score:

1. Occasionally check your credit reports for errors.
2. Pay your bills on time, especially loans and credit cards. Lenders are particularly quick to report late payments to the credit bureaus.
3. Keep your total monthly credit card charges to 10% or less of each card's credit limit. This is important, even if you plan to pay off the balance in full. Why? If you use a high percentage of your credit limit, the credit bureaus take that as a sign that you're under financial stress.
4. Don't close credit card accounts you don't use. Doing so will reduce your available credit, so your borrowing on other cards will be higher as a percentage of your remaining available credit line – and that will make you appear more financially stressed.
5. Don't apply for credit more often than is absolutely necessary and don't open too many different credit card accounts in a short space of time. If you're in the market for, say, a car loan, try to concentrate your applications within the span of a few weeks.
6. Use a mix of credit cards and car loans, mortgages or other installment loans. This can help your credit score over the long haul. But don't borrow just to raise your credit score. In the short term, that's more likely to hurt your score than help.

> If our sense of self-worth is riding on the fanciness of our car and the size of our house, peace of mind will always be a luxury.

Sometimes, we forget – and sometimes we'd rather not remember. Many of us prefer not to think about saving for the future, especially when we're lusting after some shiny new object. Meanwhile, we lose track of where we are in the month and fail to pay our bills on time. One solution to both problems: Put our financial lives on autopilot. Once we've automated our monthly finances, inertia goes from being our enemy to being our friend – and we're more likely to meet our financial commitments.

You can automate payments for all kinds of bills, including the mortgage, insurance, utilities, cell phones, cable, and more. That'll save you writing checks every month, and help you avoid late payments and the accompanying fees. Those late payments could also ding your credit score.

Keep two caveats in mind. First, make sure you always have enough in your checking account to cover these payments, or you could get whacked with overdraft, nonsufficient fund, and late payment fees. Maintaining the necessary account balance will be easier if the bills you automate don't fluctuate in size too much from one month to the next.

That brings us to the second caveat: If you automate your credit card payments, make sure you understand what's being automated. If you aren't careful, you will find that only the minimum required payment is made – which means you'll carry a balance and pay ridiculous amounts of interest. What if your credit card company will automatically tap your checking account to pay the full balance? That's better – but it also creates a risk: Given that the balance due may vary sharply from one month to the next, you need to be extra vigilant about keeping sufficient money in your checking account.

Automating your bills is helpful. Automating your investments is imperative. Without that forced savings, it's all too easy to overspend, so you reach the end of the month with little or no money socked away. Instead of spending first and saving what remains, you need to make savings the priority and then force yourself to live on whatever is left – and the way you do that is with automatic investment plans.

We've already discussed signing up to make payroll contributions to your employer's retirement plan, and also adding automatically

Day Forty

Automate It

every month to your emergency fund until you have a big enough financial cushion. But you likely have other goals, such as saving for the children's college education or for a house down payment. You should also automate these savings programs.

Let's say you hope to buy a home within the next five years. You might open a money-market mutual fund or a short-term bond fund. When you set up the account, you will likely be given the option to add automatically to the account, with the money pulled from your checking account. Go ahead and sign up, even if you can only afford to contribute $50 a month. It's a great habit to get into. You'll figure out a way to live without the money – and, fingers crossed, you will later find you can increase the sum you automatically invest each month.

- ❑ Yes, I have automated my monthly bill payments.
- ❑ Yes, I am saving and investing automatically every month for all of my goals.

If you buy stocks regularly, you buy indifference: Up markets make you richer, while down markets let you invest at cheaper prices.

Day Forty One

Added Interest

W hen we think about making our money work harder, we often focus on selecting better investments for our brokerage and retirement accounts. But we should also give some thought to how we handle our everyday cash.

On that score, consider two strategies. First, run as much of your spending as possible through a rewards credit card, so you earn cash back or travel points. Don't, however, take this as an invitation to overspend. If you end up carrying a balance, the rewards you earn likely won't come close to compensating for the interest you pay.

Second, don't leave unnecessarily large sums languishing in your checking account, where the money will earn little or no interest. A better strategy: Keep just enough cash in your checking account to cover day-to-day spending and avoid bank charges. You might move the rest into a high-yield savings account that's linked to your checking account. Back on day 19, I suggested opening a high-yield savings account to hold your emergency money. You might also use that account to hold your excess cash – or, if you prefer to keep these pools of money separate, open a second high-yield savings account.

By shifting cash into a higher-yielding account, there's the obvious advantage: You'll earn a little interest. You might use the account to hold money earmarked for, say, the mortgage or the credit card bill, and then shift the cash back to your checking account when it's time to pay these bills. Alternatively, you could arrange for the sums involved to be deducted directly from your savings account.

By getting excess cash out of your checking account, you're also less likely to fritter it away on unnecessary purchases. Many of us engage in *mental accounting*: We spend freely from our checking account, but we consider savings and investment accounts off-limits. You can turn this mindset to your advantage, by getting extra cash out of your checking account.

❑ Yes, I run as much of my spending as possible through a rewards credit card.

❑ Yes, I have moved excess cash out of my checking account and into a high-yield savings account.

> Even if their finances are a disaster waiting to happen, most folks would rather have false reassurance than the unflattering truth.

Day Forty Two

Clearing the Hurdle

It feels good when our various savings and investment accounts increase in value. But are we actually making financial progress? To answer that question, we need to consider two other factors: taxes and inflation.

Let's say we buy a bond in our taxable account that yields 4%. If we pay taxes at a 22% or 24% marginal rate, we'd lose roughly a quarter of our interest to the taxman, leaving us with an after-tax yield of 3%. That might not seem so bad – unless inflation is also 3%, in which case we're just running in place. We may feel better because our account's value has increased. But this is what's called a *money illusion*, and we are, in truth, no better off.

Yesterday, I encouraged you to move excess cash out of your checking account and into a high-yield savings account. If you'll need to spend the money soon, that's probably as much risk as you can reasonably take, and it'll allow you to earn some interest. But unfortunately, the interest you earn likely won't come close to compensating for the hit from inflation and taxes.

Instead, if you want to overcome those two threats and see your money grow over the long haul, you need to take more risk. Bonds may help you beat back the threat from inflation and taxes, especially if you buy your bonds in a tax-deferred or tax-free retirement account. But if you really want a good shot at outpacing inflation and taxes, you need to take even more risk – by going from lender to owner. That means purchasing stocks.

> The financial markets have two primary functions: to make us wealthy over time and to drive us completely batty along the way.

Day Forty Three

Be an Owner

Whether it's cars, houses, or investing, we face a major financial decision: Do we want to be an owner? With cars, that means choosing to purchase the vehicle, rather than leasing it. With housing, it's a question of buying vs. renting. With investing, we need to choose between purchasing stocks and stock funds – which makes us a part owner of the companies involved – or buying more conservative investments such as bonds, certificates of deposit and savings accounts, where we're simply lending money and receiving interest in return.

Most of us will want to be owners, assuming we have a long enough time horizon. If we want to drive a new car but plan to keep it for just three years, leasing may be the right choice. Similarly, we should probably rent a home if we can't see staying put for at least five years. Over such a short time horizon, we are unlikely to clock enough price appreciation to offset the hefty cost of first buying a house and later selling it. Ditto for stocks: If we will need our money back in less than five years, we should stick with conservative investments, because we may not have the time needed to ride out a downturn in stock prices.

But if our time horizon is longer, being an owner can make a heap of sense. Admittedly, owning a house is more of a hassle than renting and owning stocks is more nerve-racking than holding bonds. But the rewards should also be greater. By buying a house, we lock in a large part of our monthly living costs at current prices, plus we should eventually come to own a major asset free and clear. Over long holding periods, stocks have regularly delivered much better returns than bonds. What about buying cars? Almost every car depreciates. Still, by buying, we have the option to keep the car for many years – and hopefully for at least a few years after any auto loan is paid off. That'll allow us to avoid the high ongoing costs incurred by those who lease.

> Today, we worry that stocks are a bad investment. Thirty years from now, we'll wonder why we owned anything else.

Day Forty Four

All You Are

How rich are you? Think about everything you own – and everything you owe – including bank accounts, retirement accounts, car loans, credit card debt, and all the other puzzle pieces of your financial life. List them below, attaching a dollar amount to each.

What You Own	Value
TOTAL	

What You Owe	Amount

(*continued*)

TOTAL	

Take the value of your assets and subtract your debts:

NET WORTH	

When calculating a client's net worth, financial advisors will include auto loans and credit card debt, but not the possessions that were bought were these debts. Why not? Your car, furniture, and most other household effects will depreciate and eventually become worthless. Maybe more important, if you were in a financial pinch, you couldn't really sell these possessions. After all, where would you sit and how would get around town?

Some financial advisors go a step further, counting mortgage debt as a liability, but only part of the value of a client's house as an asset – and only if the client plans to trade down to a smaller place when he or she retires, thereby freeing up home equity. It's the same rationale that's used to exclude possessions: You need to live somewhere, so a home can't really be sold to generate spending money (though, once retired, you might consider a reverse mortgage).

Want to see the truly big picture? You can make this analysis even more sophisticated by including the cost of your goals among your liabilities. Need $1 million to retire in comfort and $200,000 to put your two kids through state universities? You would add $1.2 million to your liabilities.

Starting to feel poor? If you're going to include the cost of your goals among your liabilities, it's only fair that you also give yourself credit for a major asset – your human capital. Depending on your occupation, when you're in your twenties, your future earning power might be worth anywhere from $1.5 million (think clerical worker) to $5 million or more (think lawyer). That earning power will provide the savings you need to pay for your life's goals.

> If our net worth was displayed on our foreheads for all to see, libraries would be mobbed and used cars would be status symbols.

Day Forty Five

Riding the Life Cycle

Two days ago, we discussed the virtues of being an owner. Yesterday, we tallied your assets and liabilities. How should all this change over your lifetime?

When we start adult life, we might have substantial student loans and little or nothing in savings. But we also have four decades of paychecks ahead of us. When we reach retirement, we will have no more paychecks, but – if all has gone well – also no debt, a house we own, and a hefty pile of savings. Those savings might be in a mix of stocks and bonds.

What happens in between? Initially, the debts can pile up thick and fast. On top of any student loans, we might take out an auto loan to buy a car and a mortgage to purchase a house. Obviously, we need to be careful not to borrow too much. But taking on debt can be a smart strategy, because it helps us jumpstart our financial lives, and we know we have decades of paychecks ahead of us to whittle down these debts.

As we take on debt early in our adult lives, we should also start saving for the future. How should we invest those dollars? If we have goals that are more than five years away – think retirement and our toddler's college education – the money should be largely in stocks. That might seem risky.

But if we look at our broad financial picture, the risk involved is modest. The amount of money in our portfolio is probably tiny compared to the paychecks we hope to collect. Those paychecks will likely provide us with a fairly steady stream of income, so we have less need for bonds and other more conservative investments, which are bought principally for their stable value and regular interest payments.

On top of that, we will be regularly saving a part of those future paychecks. That'll allow us to buy stocks at all kinds of different prices, some high, some low. What if the stock market crashes? That might sound like bad news, but it could prove to be a bonanza, because we can buy shares at rock-bottom prices. In short, for much of our adult lives, not only do we have the necessary time horizon to clock healthy stock market gains, but also there's little need to own conservative investments, because we don't need income from our portfolio.

That changes as we approach retirement. Our paycheck is about to disappear and soon we will need to start pulling money from our portfolio. That means we should probably keep roughly half our money in conservative investments, with the other half in stocks to provide continued growth. With our paycheck disappearing, it also becomes harder to service debt, so we'll want to avoid further borrowing and pay off any loans we already have.

Most of us begin adult life with little money, but much time – an advantage that can transform small sums into impressive wealth.

Day Forty Six

Taking Aim

We have taken a close look at your everyday spending and at the large purchases you hope to make in the years ahead, and we have tried to make sure you're committing your dollars to the things that matter most to you. Now, it's time to tackle the biggest ticket items: your long-term goals.

Often, we have just three long-term goals: retirement, college for the kids, and buying a home. But you might have others, such as a second home or a major remodeling project that may take many years to save for. Below, list your long-term goals, set a target date, and estimate how much each will cost. Include a few additional details, such as where you hope to retire, what sort of house you'd like to buy, and which college you want your children to attend. These extra details can bring your goals to life – and help fuel your motivation.

Goal	When	Cost	Additional Details

If we don't know where we're headed with our financial lives, we'll likely end up somewhere we don't like.

Day Forty Seven

The Last Shall Be First

Y ou have now nailed down your long-term goals. But what should your priorities be? That's an easy one. Chronologically, retirement may be the last of our life goals, but we should always put it first – because it's the only goal that isn't optional.

No, we don't have to buy a house. No, we don't have to pay for our children's college education. But unless we suffer an early demise, one day we will almost certainly retire, and that will involve a heap of dollars. To amass the necessary sum, we need to make saving for retirement a priority throughout our working career.

I realize this seems backward. Why prioritize retirement – which might be years away – when we could be focusing on buying a home and paying the kids' college tuition bills, which are coming up all too quickly? Many folks postpone saving for retirement while they focus on these more immediate goals, and it's a huge mistake. If we put off saving for retirement until our late thirties or even our forties, we will be hard-pressed to save enough for a comfortable retirement, unless we can find some way to sock away 20% of our income every year and perhaps much more. Indeed, if we procrastinate too long, there may be no way to make the numbers work, and suddenly we might be faced with an impoverished retirement or a working career that lasts far longer than we ever imagined.

My advice: As soon as you enter the workforce, begin contributing to your employer's retirement plan or start funding an individual retirement account, and preferably both. This can be a tall task – you'll likely be on a modest income and perhaps paying back student loans – but the potential benefits are enormous. Every dollar you sock away could enjoy decades of investment compounding, making it far easier to amass the hefty sum needed for a decent retirement.

What about saving for a house down payment and putting aside money for the kids' college education? Both are worthy goals, and you should shoot for them if you can – but not at the expense of your own retirement.

> The best time to start saving and investing for retirement has already passed. The next best time is today.

Day Forty Eight

Marking Time

I magine your perfect retirement day. How would you spend your morning, afternoon, and evening? List the things you might do from the time you wake up until you head to bed:

No doubt you would be happy spending a week or two following this schedule. But would you be happy doing these things every day for the rest of your life? Many retirees suffer from vacation confusion. They treat retirement like a long holiday, and quickly become bored and even depressed, as they discover that endless fun and relaxation isn't all that satisfying. Instead, they hanker for the days when their lives had a greater sense of purpose.

You might be thinking, "Why are you bothering me with this? I'm years from retirement."

That might be true. But you should think ahead to retirement for the same reason you should look back to the happiest times in your life. By doing so, you can get a handle on what you really enjoy – and that might provide a roadmap not just for retirement but also for hobbies and alternative careers in the years ahead. You want to identify activities that you are passionate about, find challenging, consider important, and believe you're good at.

When we are engaged in such activities, we can find ourselves in the psychological state known as *flow*. We are totally absorbed by what we're doing and the time just whizzes by. We might not be having fun in the conventional sense, and yet these can be among our happiest times.

Such activities can propel us out of bed in the morning and give a sense of purpose to our days, both during our working years and when we are retired. In fact, I'd like to see the distinction between work and retirement disappear. Instead, we should view one as a continuation of the other: In retirement, we should keep the focus on activities we find fulfilling, but without the constraint of having to earn an income.

Got activities you can't wait to devote more time to? With any luck, that'll inspire you to get your financial house in order as quickly as possible – so you have the financial freedom to live the life you want.

> We spend decades preparing financially for retirement – and yet we often give scant thought to what we'll do with all that free time.

Day Forty Nine

Calling It Quits

How much money do you need for a comfortable retirement? Here's the quick-and-dirty calculation: Take your current pretax annual income and multiply it by 12. Let's say you make $50,000 a year. For retirement, you'll want a net worth of around $600,000, defined as all money in financial accounts minus any debt.

What's the logic behind this calculation? One popular rule of thumb says that, in the first year of retirement, you can withdraw 4% of your portfolio's value and thereafter step up your annual withdrawals with inflation. Take that $600,000. A 4% withdrawal rate – equal to $4,000 for every $100,000 saved – would give you $24,000 for the first year of your retirement. That's almost half of the $50,000 annual income we assumed you were making.

On top of that, you will likely also receive Social Security. The typical Social Security benefit runs around $16,000 a year. Add that to the $24,000 from your portfolio, and you'd have $40,000 a year for retirement. Typically, Social Security replaces a higher percentage of your income from your working years if you were lower paid. If that's the case, you might be okay with a somewhat smaller nest egg – maybe eight times your current pretax annual income.

Similarly, if you'll receive a traditional employer pension, which will pay you monthly income in retirement, you might be safe amassing somewhat less. Let's say you are eligible for not just Social Security but also a pension that will replicate a quarter of your salary. To supplement that, you might aim for a nest egg equal to six times your current income.

Even with Social Security and perhaps a pension, you will probably retire with less income than you had when you were working. But remember, your expenses will likely also come down. Once you retire, you won't need to save for retirement any more, plus you won't be paying Social Security and Medicare payroll taxes. Together, those might have been eating up 20% of your income. With any luck, if you own your home, you'll also have the mortgage paid off by retirement, which will further trim your living costs.

Now that you have seen how the math plays out, ask yourself:

❏ What multiple of income do I need saved by retirement?

❏ What does that mean in dollars? $

To find out if you're on track to amass your target retirement amount, head to Calculator.net and use the Investment Calculator. Click on the tab for "End Amount" and insert how many years until you hope to retire, how much you currently have saved for retirement, and the total amount you sock away each month in your various retirement accounts. Assume a 2% return. This might seem low. But remember, we need to make allowances for both inflation and investment costs.

Falling short? You could save more each month, push back your retirement date by a few years, settle for a more frugal retirement, or consider some combination thereof. What's your plan?

It might be ideal to save just enough every month for retirement. The reality is messier: We retire with whatever we've amassed – and the more we have, the better.

Can you afford the house of your dreams? Do you have the where-withal to pay for your children's college education? Is it financially prudent to take the two-week European vacation? I'm not here to tell you how to spend your money. As far as I'm concerned, you can use your dollars however you wish – as long as you're taking care of your future self and those financially dependent on you.

That means making sure you save enough each month for retirement. You also need at least four other tools in your financial toolbox: an emergency plan in case you lose your job, health insurance, disability insurance if you have less than $1 million in savings, and term life insurance if you have less than $1 million in savings and a family that depends on you financially. Got all that nailed down? The other financial choices are all yours.

With any luck, once you've taken care of your financial needs, you'll have some financial wiggle room – and you can devote dollars to things you want. That's why we've spent so much time focusing on what you enjoy most about your daily life and what you want from the future.

So what do you value? Some folks will want to use their financial wiggle room to buy a home or even a second home. Others will want fancy colleges for their kids or fancy cars for themselves. Yet others will want to devote their spare dollars to special trips or a more lavish daily lifestyle. None of these is a bad choice – as long as they are what you truly want and they don't come at the expense of your future self.

Many folks consider it virtuous to have a monthly budget and track their daily spending. If you struggle to live within your means and look after your future self, that's probably necessary. But if you are socking away enough for the future and taking the necessary precautions in case of bad times, I wouldn't worry too much about budgeting and tracking your spending. The goal here is remarkably simple: You want to save enough today so you have sufficient

Day Fifty

Needs First, Wants Second

spending money in the future – while spending today on things you truly value.

❑ Yes, I'm taking the necessary steps to take care of my family and my future self.

> Luxury cars. But are they leased? Huge home. But how big is the mortgage? Beautiful garden. But has the landscaper been paid?

Day Fifty One

Getting Real about Real Estate

I think everybody should aim to become a homeowner, because it's a great way to lock in your housing costs and eventually eliminate them. True, if you own a home, you will face rising property taxes, rising premiums for homeowner's insurance, and frequent bills for maintenance and repairs, and those costs will never go away.

But your core cost – your mortgage's monthly principal-and-interest payment – won't ever rise if you take out a fixed-rate mortgage and, indeed, it should become more affordable as your salary climbs along with inflation and any merit increases. If you opt for an adjustable-rate mortgage, you'll face a little more uncertainty, but your inflation-adjusted monthly mortgage payment should also shrink over time.

Even better, once the mortgage is paid off, that'll be the end of a major monthly expense. Renters get no such relief: They face endless and ever-rising monthly payments.

Still, while owning a house can be a smart move, don't get carried away and buy a ridiculously large home. There is no virtue in owning a house that's bigger than your family needs. To understand why, think about the gain from homeownership in two parts.

First, there's the price appreciation. Over the long haul, this may be slightly ahead of inflation, before factoring in costs. But once you subtract maintenance, property taxes, and insurance, your home's price gain will likely lag far behind inflation – and you could be losing money. The upshot: If you buy an overly large house, you're betting big on an investment that will deliver little in the way of price appreciation.

Fortunately, the gain from homeownership includes a second component: the *imputed rent*. What's that? If you live in your own home, you are effectively renting to yourself – which means you're getting a lot of value from the house. How much value? Think about how much you could collect each year if you rented out your house, and how that annual rent compares to your home's current value. There's a good chance this annual imputed rent is equal to 6% or 7% of your home's value.

The bottom line: A home's imputed rent is worth far more than the price appreciation that homeowners love to boast about. What's the financial implication? If you're purchasing a home, or trading up to a large place, you should aim to buy a house that's big enough for you and your family, but no bigger. If you purchase an overly large house, you're throwing away money. It's like renting a huge place, but only using half the rooms.

Tempted to sell stocks and buy rental real estate? Remember, stocks don't call at 2 a.m. complaining that the toilet's clogged.

Day Fifty Two

Homeward Bound

T hinking of buying a home or trading up to a larger place? Here's the financial checklist:

❑ Yes, buying makes sense, because I can see staying put for at least five years, and preferably seven years or longer.

> If your time horizon is any shorter, you could lose money if the market turns lower and you have to sell before prices recover. Even if you benefit from rising property prices, any gain could be offset by the costs you incur buying and later selling the house.

❑ Yes, I've checked my credit reports and credit score, so I know I'll look like a worthy borrower to mortgage lenders.

> It's best to check your credit reports and credit score at least six months before applying for a mortgage, so you have time to fix mistakes in your reports and take steps to improve your score.

❑ Yes, I have enough for a house down payment or I've start socking away the necessary money.

> To avoid the cost of private mortgage insurance, try to make a 20% down payment. Even if you can't put down 20%, the larger your down payment, the better. Until you buy a house, you might keep the money for your future down payment in a money-market mutual fund or a high-yield savings account.

❑ Yes, I've gauged how much I might be able to borrow by heading to HSH.com and using the "How Much House Can I Afford?" calculator.

> As a rule, lenders will let you take on mortgage payments, including property taxes and home-owner's insurance, that equal 28% of your pretax monthly income.

❑ Yes, I realize I'll face other purchase costs, including legal fees, title insurance, moving expenses, mortgage application fees, and more, so I'm saving extra money to cover those bills.

> While buying is costly, selling is even more expensive, thanks to the 5% or 6% real-estate brokerage commission you'll likely pay. This is one reason you need to own a house for at least five years, so there's a chance for price appreciation to offset the steep cost of first buying a home and later selling it.

Want to hurt your happiness? Buy a big house involving lots of upkeep and a long commute.

Day Fifty Three

The Kids Are All Right

Are there children – either your own or somebody else's – whom you'd like to help financially? If so, what sort of assistance do you want to provide? List the children you would like to help, which goals you're looking to help with, and how much you are willing to commit, either as a lump sum or a monthly investment.

Who	Why	How Much

You might be aiming to help with a house down payment or a car purchase. But in all likelihood, the biggest-ticket item is college costs. If that's on your list, it's important to figure out the best way to help. Here's a simple way to think about it:

❖ If you're one of the parents and your combined income is less than $100,000, there's some chance your child could receive financial aid, so you should probably focus on shoring up your own finances by building up retirement accounts, buying a home, and paying down debt. These steps will get you in good financial shape, so you'll be better able to help with college costs once the bills start rolling in – plus, they shouldn't hurt your aid eligibility.

❖ If you aren't one of the parents – but the parents' income is less than $100,000 – you should keep the money earmarked for college costs in your own name, and then make financial gifts to the parents once the child involved is in college.

❖ If you're one of the parents and your combined income is $100,000 or above, there's less chance of financial aid, so set up a 529 college savings plan and sock away money regularly. If you aren't the parents – but the parents have income of $100,000 and up – contribute to a 529 set up by the parents. Money in a 529 plan grows tax-free, provided it's used to pay qualified education expenses, and accounts owned by the parents are least likely to create financial-aid headaches.

When picking a 529 plan, first see if there's a state tax break for funding an in-state plan. To find out, head to SavingforCollege.com. If there isn't a state tax break – or if your state's plan has high costs – consider buying Vanguard Group's low-cost 529 plan, which is sponsored by the state of Nevada and available through Vanguard.com.

> Is it time to have the talk with your kids? You know, the important one – about how much you'll help with college costs.

Day Fifty Four

Compounding for Life

Back on day 6, we discussed compounding. At the time, I noted that, if you invested $1,000 and earned 6% a year, you would have $5,743 after 30 years. But what if the $1,000 was left to grow for twice as long – and what if that growth was tax-free? After 60 years, you would have $32,988 to spend in any way you wish.

That brings me to one of the great financial gifts you can make to teenagers or those in their twenties. If they have earned income – meaning they have a job that's paying them income – help them to fund a Roth IRA. The maximum contribution is either their annual earnings or that year's legal limit ($5,500 in 2018), whichever is lower. With a Roth, there's no upfront tax deduction. But in return for giving up that immediate tax break, you get not-tax-deferred growth – meaning the money will eventually be taxed – but rather tax-free growth.

A teenager could easily get six decades of tax-free growth out of a Roth, and perhaps more. And if you get the Roth opened, your favorite teenager might continue to contribute every year – and the account could be worth well over $1 million by retirement. Keep in mind that if someone's income is too high, he or she can't fund a Roth, but that's unlikely to be an issue for young adults early in their career.

Want to make sure your teenager has some skin in the game? You could make this offer: You'll contribute a dollar for every dollar the teenager contributes. If that seems too onerous, you could make it two or even three dollars for every dollar the kid kicks in. When you open the account, you should take the chance to talk about investing, the virtues of the Roth IRA, and the specific investments you have chosen.

Intrigued? List the teenagers or young adults you'd like to get started on a lifetime of investing:

_____

_____

_____

_____

_____

_____

_____

_____

_____

_____

_____

If we don't educate our children about money, one day a broker will teach them lessons they'll never forget.

Day Fifty Five

History Lesson

Today, we'll look at your experience as an investor. Start with two thoughts. First, the best predictor of our future behavior is our past behavior. Second, we misremember the past.

In truth, "misremember" is too polite. We often believe our investments performed far better than they really did. We imagine that we foresaw major market developments. We might even remember bravely buying during a market decline, when we were, in fact, panicked and selling. We lie to ourselves all the time – and yet we don't even know we're lying.

All this makes it hard to become better investors. Want to get a handle on how smart you have been and the mistakes you've made? Forget your recollections and look at the evidence:

❖ If your brokerage firm, 401(k) provider or mutual-fund company calculates your personal rate of return, see how it compares to major market indexes. For instance, you might compare your personal rate of return to the performance of Vanguard Group's total stock market index fund and its total bond market index fund. Make sure you're looking at performance over the same time period. Does your personal performance look weak? Perhaps you should stop trying to pick winning investments and instead purchase index funds that simply track the market's performance.

❖ If you were investing in late 2008 and early 2009, when global stock markets collapsed, grab your old account statements and see whether you were buying stocks or selling. If you were a seller, that suggests your risk tolerance is low – and you should probably favor a more conservative portfolio.

❖ Look at how many stock and stock fund sales you've made over the past year. A handful of sales could mean you needed cash or you were tweaking your portfolio to keep it in line with your target investment mix. But if there were a lot of sales, it likely reflects frequent changes of heart about your investment strategy – a sign that perhaps you aren't sure what you are doing.

Stocks will fluctuate today, whether we look or not.

Day Fifty Six

Fear Factor

When we invest for distant goals like retirement or our toddler's college education, we need to weigh two major risks. First, there's the risk that we invest too conservatively, and end up with modest returns that fail to fend off the twin threats of inflation and taxes. Second, there's the risk that we invest too aggressively and find ourselves petrified by the next large market decline and perhaps even fleeing stocks at the worst possible time.

The second risk is potentially far more damaging. If we freak out during a market crash and sell at fire-sale prices, the financial cost could be devastating. Yesterday, we looked at your investment experience. Do you have a history of jumping from one investment to the next? If so, you should probably steer clear of individual stocks. Instead, favor mutual funds – especially those that offer broad market exposure – and lean toward a more conservative portfolio.

What if you have little or no experience as an investor? Until you have a better handle on your tolerance for risk, it's wise to err on the side of caution and hold a somewhat more conservative portfolio, perhaps splitting your money between stock and bond funds. If you get a few years of stock market investing under your belt and feel you can stomach more risk, you might increase your allocation to stocks.

- ❑ On a scale from 1 to 10, where 10 would suggest you're utterly fearless, how would you rate your risk tolerance?

- ❑ On a scale from 1 to 10, where 10 would indicate you're an extremely knowledge investor with a consistent investment philosophy, how would you rate your investment competence?

Now, ask yourself: Does your portfolio reflect how you view your own risk tolerance and sophistication, or are you being too aggressive or too clever?

> If tumbling markets don't excite you, investing will always be fraught with anxiety, and success will likely prove elusive.

Day Fifty Seven

It's All in the Mix

The key driver of both our portfolio's short-term price swings and its likely long-run return is our so-called *asset allocation*. What's that? It's our basic mix of four investment categories: stocks, bonds, cash investments like money-market funds and savings accounts, and alternative investments such as gold, real estate, and hedge funds.

Stocks are undoubtedly risky in the short-term, but they can be a portfolio's engine of growth over the long haul, generating gains that easily outstrip inflation. Cash investments almost always prove to be low risk, but there's a strong likelihood they'll lose us money once inflation and taxes are factored in.

What about bonds and alternative investments? Most bonds would count as a conservative investment, kicking off a steady stream of interest without too much fluctuation in price. But some can give investors a wild ride, including high-yield junk bonds, emerging market debt, and Treasury bonds with 20 or more years to maturity.

Similarly, alternative investments are a mixed bag. The hope with alternative investments is that they'll post gains when the stock market is falling. But they don't always deliver on that promise – and many suffer wild price fluctuations. That's why investors often limit alternatives to 10% of their portfolio's value and some avoid the category entirely.

You should have a target asset allocation for each of your major goals. For instance, if you plan to buy a house in the next three years, you can't afford to take a lot of risk, so your target allocation should probably be 100% cash investments. But if you're investing for a retirement that is 30 years away, your target might be 90% stocks and 10% bonds.

Below, list your major goals. For each one, write down your target asset allocation – what percentage you'll invest in stocks, bonds, cash investments, and alternative investments:

Goal	Investment Mix			
	% Stocks	% Bonds	% Cash	% Alternatives

Our precise mix of stocks, bonds, cash, and alternative investments is less important than our willingness to stick with it.

Day Fifty Eight

Spreading Your Bets

Once you settle on your asset allocation for any particular goal, the next step is to diversify – and that means buying lots and lots of securities.

Admittedly, this isn't so important with cash investments. If you have a money market mutual fund, there isn't a strong *diversification* argument for opening a high-yield savings account. Instead, diversification matters most with bonds, alternative investments, and stocks.

Let's say you own shares in just one company. What if that company gets into financial trouble? There's every chance you'll lose much or all of your investment, no matter how well the rest of the stock market is performing. You'll have taken a massive amount of risk – making a big bet on a single company – and yet have nothing to show for it.

To avoid that fate, you need to own lots of stocks – big and small, US and foreign. Similarly, you'll want to own lots of different bonds and, if you opt to invest in alternative investments, you should buy many different securities. By diversifying broadly, you reduce the risk of owning any particular stock or bond, and you are far more likely to be rewarded for the risk you're taking. In other words, if you are diversified and the financial markets rise over time, your portfolio will almost certainly go along for the ride.

Buying so many stocks and bonds might sound daunting. In truth, it's remarkably easy – thanks to mutual funds and exchange-traded index funds. Funds simply bundle together a bunch of different stocks, bonds, and other investments into a single package, making it easy for investors to get broad market exposure with a relatively modest investment. Take the Vanguard Total World Stock Index Fund, which owns some 8,000 stocks from every part of the global market. That's extraordinary diversification – and yet it takes just $3,000 to open an account.

> It's amazing how much our portfolios can grow when we aren't looking – and how that abruptly stops when we meddle.

Day Fifty Nine

Reducing Drag

Dazzled by the prospect of big gains, investors often give far too little thought to investment costs. But if we aren't careful, we could find ourselves paying annual costs equal to 2% of our portfolio's value, and perhaps much more. We could hit that 2% if we buy high-expense mutual funds, purchase insurance products positioned as investments, trade too much, or hire a broker or financial advisor who steers us toward higher-cost products.

Admittedly, paying 2% of our portfolio's value each year might not sound so bad – which is why Wall Street likes to frame investment costs that way. But that 2% could be devouring a huge chunk of each year's potential investment return. Let's say the stock market returns 6% a year. If we pay 2% in investment costs, our net return will be 4%. That means a third of our potential return disappeared into Wall Street's pocket.

Your task for today: Figure out what you pay to invest.

Given the importance of keeping investment costs to a minimum, this is much harder than it ought to be. With some investments, like a savings account, certificate of deposit, fixed annuity, or cash-value life insurance, there's no stated expense ratio. That doesn't mean these products are cheap. In particular, almost all investments that are sold by insurance companies pay high commissions to the salespeople involved and effectively levy high ongoing costs. But this, alas, isn't clearly disclosed to investors – and it may not be disclosed at all.

Other investments – such as buying individual stocks and bonds – can appear deceptively cheap, because you might pay little or nothing in commissions. But the big hit is the trading spread on individual stocks and the markup on individual bonds. Every stock and bond has two prices: the higher price at which you can currently buy and the lower price at which you can sell. The spread or markup represents the difference between those two prices, but it's tough for everyday investors to figure what that difference is.

Yet other investments – notably, mutual funds, including those in your employer's retirement plan – make clear what commission, if any, is levied when you buy and sell, as well as how much you pay in ongoing annual expenses. Ideally, you want to own funds that are no-load, meaning there's no commission when you buy or sell, and which have annual expenses of less than 0.5%, equal to 50 cents a year for every $100 you have invested. The lower the expenses are, the better.

Below, list the investments you own and how much they cost to buy and sell, as well as what sort of ongoing expense is involved. If you can't figure out the cost, you can write N.A., or not available. If there are a lot of N.A.s, that's a warning sign – and it could mean you are paying far more to invest than you realize.

Investment	Cost to Buy	Ongoing Cost	Cost to Sell

When we buy an investment, we can't be sure we have a winner. But if we hold down costs, we will at least keep more of whatever we make.

Day Sixty

Cutting Taxes

As you seek to hold down investment costs, you should also pay attention to the biggest investment cost of all – taxes. How do you do that? Follow four simple rules.

First, make the most of tax-favored retirement accounts. A 401(k) or similar employer-sponsored retirement plan can give you the investor's triple play: an immediate tax deduction, tax-deferred growth and a matching employer contribution. If you qualify, a traditional IRA can give you the double play: a tax deduction and tax-deferred growth.

What about a Roth IRA or Roth 401(k)? There's no immediate tax deduction, but money withdrawn in retirement can be totally tax-free. By contrast, with non-Roth retirement accounts, you have to pay income taxes when you make withdrawals. Tax-deductible accounts make the most sense if you expect to be taxed at a lower rate once retired, while Roth accounts are more appealing if you expect your tax bracket in retirement to be the same or higher.

Second rule: Avoid earning a lot of interest income in your regular taxable account. Interest income – such as the income kicked off by bonds and savings accounts – is immediately taxable at your marginal income tax rate (though interest from some federal government bonds isn't taxable at the state level and interest from municipal bonds may be completely tax-free). Do you pay tax at, say, a 12%, 22%, or 24% rate on any additional dollars you earn? That's your marginal tax rate – and that's the cut that Uncle Sam takes of any interest you earn.

Third, minimize trading in your regular taxable account. If you sell investments in your taxable account and realize a profit, you'll have to pay taxes on that capital gain – and the tax rate can be especially steep if you held the investment for a year or less. Keep in mind that you need to worry not just about your own trading but also about any trading by the mutual funds you hold in your taxable account. This is a reason to hold stock index funds in your taxable account. Stock index funds simply buy and hold the stocks that make up a market index, so they tend to generate relatively modest tax bills.

Finally, never have a year when you pay no taxes. If you have just retired or you're out of work, you might have a tax year when you owe little or nothing to Uncle Sam. This is a wasted opportunity. How so? You could use a year like that to realize investment gains or convert part of a traditional IRA to a Roth IRA, and pay relatively little in taxes.

> Taxes are the price of success – but there's no need to boast too much in front of Uncle Sam.

Day Sixty One

Worth the Wait

Yesterday, we discussed the importance of both funding retirement accounts and limiting the amount you trade in your regular taxable account. In many cases, these two strategies are simply delaying the day of reckoning: When you make withdrawals from most retirement accounts and when you sell a profitable investment that's held in your taxable account, you have to pay taxes.

Still, the longer you can delay paying those taxes, the more money you stand to make. Think of it this way: If you have money sitting in a traditional 401(k) plan or you have a stock in your taxable account that's been a profitable investment, the taxman has a claim on a slice of your money. But if you can put off paying the taxman his share, you can use that money to earn additional gains for yourself.

How valuable is this tax deferral? Consider a husband and wife. They both invest $1,000 in the same investment, but he buys it in a taxable account and she purchases it in a traditional, tax-deferred retirement account that doesn't offer an initial tax deduction. Over the next 40 years, the investment climbs 6% a year.

The husband pays taxes on his entire 6% gain every year at a 24% rate. The wife also pays taxes at 24%, but she doesn't pay taxes on her gain until she cashes in her retirement account, 40 years after she made the initial investment. Result? The husband amasses $5,951, while the wife walks away with $8,057, or 35% more.

> To add to our wealth, we should focus on minimizing the subtractions: taxes, investment costs and foolish financial bets.

Day Sixty Two

Everything
in Its Place

Two days ago, I offered four rules for managing your investment tax bill. Yesterday, we discussed the benefits of deferring taxes. What's the implication of all this? You should think carefully about which investments you hold in your tax-favored retirement accounts and which in your regular taxable account. The reason: With some investments and investment strategies, you can lose a quarter or more of each year's investment gains to the taxman. With others, you lose little or nothing.

For instance, a corporate bond will kick off interest every year that's taxable – and the tax is assessed at the income tax rate, rather than at the lower capital gains rate. Under current tax law, so-called ordinary income can be taxed at federal rates as high as 37%. That's almost double the rate levied on long-term capital gains and qualified dividends, which are taxed at 20% or less.

Similarly, if you trade stocks quickly, so your holding period is a year or less, any gains won't qualify for the long-term capital gains rate. Instead, you'll have to pay tax at the much higher rate levied on ordinary income.

By contrast, other investments and strategies generate little or nothing in annual taxes. Let's say you buy and hold individual stocks or stock index mutual funds. Because you aren't doing any trading, you won't trigger capital gains taxes – and because most index funds don't actively trade their portfolios, they should pay out little or nothing in capital gains distributions. True, you may receive dividends. But those should be taxed at a special low rate.

What does all this mean for your portfolio? You should use your taxable account to pursue strategies that generate modest annual tax bills, while restricting high-tax strategies to your retirement accounts. Here's how that might work in practice:

―――――――――――――――― ∽ ――――――――――――――――

Taxable Account
❖ Stock index funds
❖ Buy-and-hold individual stocks
❖ Tax-free municipal bonds and bond funds

Retirement Account

❖ Actively managed stock funds

❖ Trading individual stocks

❖ Taxable bonds and bond funds

❖ Real estate investment trusts

Ponder your own portfolio. Do you have the right investments in the right account?

An important caveat: You shouldn't necessarily pursue all the strategies listed above. I don't think it's wise to trade individual stocks or buy actively managed mutual funds, because the track record for these strategies isn't good. But if you're going to do so, a retirement account is your best bet, so you don't end up wreaking havoc on your tax return.

For the past three days, we've discussed investment taxes. Are there adjustments you ought to make? Make a list of potential portfolio changes:

_____

_____

_____

_____

_____

_____

_____

If you weren't burdened by the knowledge of what you hold, what you sold, and how markets have fared, would you own your current portfolio?

Day Sixty Three

Unbeatable

Imagine you joined a bunch of weekend warriors facing off against a professional basketball team. Or you found yourself on the other side of the court from a Wimbledon champion. Or you pulled your old bike out of the garage and lined up for the start of the Tour de France. What do you think your chances of success would be? This isn't exactly a tough question: The odds of coming out on top are probably somewhere between zero and nothing.

Investing is no different.

Reams of statistics and undeniable logic have firmly established that investing is a loser's game. The vast majority of investors – both amateurs and professionals – earn results that trail the market averages. It couldn't be otherwise. Before investment costs, we collectively earn the return of the stock and bond markets. After costs, we must inevitably earn less.

Sure, there are always a few winners, just as there's always somebody who wins the lottery. You may even beat the stock market averages this year and perhaps next. But the relentless tyranny of investment costs will eventually take their toll – and your chances of outpacing the market over a lifetime of investing probably aren't much better than your chances of beating a professional tennis player. In fact, the odds may be worse: While a professional tennis player can have a bad day, the stock market is always fiercely competitive.

This is a notion that many folks are reluctant to accept. Our unreliable memories trick us into believing our investments have performed better than they really have. In our overconfidence, we feel certain we know which stocks will soar and which way the market is headed next. But these delusions are costly – and the sooner we accept that we're unlikely to beat the market, the brighter our financial future will be.

> Wall Street feeds the fantasy that we can beat the market, because the fantasy is a great moneymaker – for Wall Street.

Day Sixty Four

Matching the Market

Y ou're now ready to pick investments. Over the past week, we've talked about your asset allocation – your basic mix of stocks and more conservative investments. We've looked at the importance of diversifying broadly and holding down investment costs, including taxes. We've discussed how unlikely it is that you'll beat the market.

What does all this mean for the investments you buy? Even folks who agree on the fundamentals of investing end up with all kinds of different portfolios. But let me suggest two super-simple strategies. We'll discuss one today and one tomorrow.

Today's suggestion: Build a portfolio using three core index funds. Index funds buy many or all of the securities that make up a market index, in an effort to match the index's performance. The funds almost always fall slightly short of this goal, because of their investment expenses. Still, those expenses are typically low, so the shortfall is modest – and far less than that suffered by most active investors, with their much higher investment costs. Result: By aiming for average, index funds fare far better than most other strategies.

Index funds come in two varieties: mutual funds and exchange-traded funds (ETFs). Mutual funds are bought directly from the fund companies involved, with their share price established as of the 4 p.m. ET market close. Exchange-traded funds are listed on the stock market and are available for purchase throughout the trading day. To buy shares, you need to open a brokerage account.

You might build a portfolio by combining three index funds: a total US stock market index fund, a total US bond market index fund and a total international stock index fund. These three funds are available as mutual funds from Fidelity Investments and Vanguard Group, for example, and as ETFs managed by iShares, SPDRs, and Vanguard.

Charles Schwab also offers index mutual funds and ETFs that invest in all three sectors, though its broad international fund includes only developed markets. That means you'd probably want to add a fourth fund devoted to emerging markets. Nonetheless, Schwab's funds are notable for their low costs, plus Schwab's mutual funds require just a $1 minimum initial investment.

How should you divvy up your money among these three funds? You might put $6 in a total US stock market index fund for every $4 you put in a total international stock index fund. How about bonds? That depends on how much risk you can stomach and how far off your goals lie. The closer you are to your goals – and the queasier you are about stock market swings – the more you should invest in the total bond market index fund. Aim to hold that bond fund in your retirement account, so you don't have to pay taxes each year on the interest you earn.

> There are those who think they're investment geniuses – and then there are those smart enough to index.

Day Sixty Five

One-Stop Shopping

Yesterday, we discussed combining three index funds to create a globally diversified portfolio. For today, I promised a second approach – and this one is even simpler. Instead of combining three index funds, you might purchase a single target-date retirement fund.

A target-date fund provides a broadly diversified portfolio in a single fund, with each fund geared toward a particular retirement date. For instance, a fund targeting 2045 would have a mix of stocks and bonds that would be appropriate for someone turning age 65 in 2045 or thereabouts.

The big advantage of target-date funds is their simplicity. Indeed, they have become a mainstay of many 401(k) plans and may even be the default investment option. But there are drawbacks. While most target-date funds don't charge any expenses themselves, they typically invest in other funds offered by the sponsoring fund company – and these funds can be costly and will almost always be actively managed.

Three exceptions: Charles Schwab, Fidelity Investments and Vanguard Group all have a series of target-date retirement funds that invest in each company's own index funds. That means the funds have low annual expenses, 0.08% a year for the Schwab funds, 0.15% for Fidelity's offerings and 0.13% to 0.15% for the Vanguard funds. Keep in mind that, while the stock index portion of these funds shouldn't generate big tax bills, you will owe income taxes each year on the interest kicked off by the bonds – assuming you hold your target-date fund in a regular taxable account, rather than a retirement account. Also keep in mind that Fidelity and Schwab have a separate series of target-date funds that invest in actively managed funds, and those funds have much higher annual expenses.

Even if you would like to own just three index funds or just one target-date fund, that probably won't be possible. You might end up with a 401(k) plan, an individual retirement account, and a regular taxable account. Your spouse might have the same selection of accounts, plus you might also have 529 plans for the kids. In each of these accounts, you'll need to hold at least one investment.

Moreover, your 401(k) might have neither target-date funds nor index funds. You'll be left to muddle through, perhaps building a globally diversified portfolio with actively managed funds you aren't that enthusiastic about. Still, look for the lower-cost options, and be sure to diversify broadly.

So what's your plan? Make your selection:

- ❏ I'm going to build my own portfolio using three broad market index funds.
- ❏ I'm going to buy a target-date retirement fund.
- ❏ I have another investment strategy in mind. Here's what I plan to do:

_____

_____

_____

_____

_____

_____

_____

Global markets consist of four key sectors: US stocks, US bonds, foreign stocks, and foreign bonds. Own just one? You're making a huge bet.

Day Sixty Six

Coping with Crazy Markets

Buying stocks and stock funds is easy. Staying invested is the struggle. We may be managing money for a retirement that is decades away – and that might last two or three decades beyond that – and yet most of us pay close attention to the stock market's daily performance, especially at times of market turmoil. The danger: We get so unnerved by a market downturn that we end up selling at the worst possible time.

With any luck, you'll grow more comfortable with the stock market over time. But these three strategies may help:

❖ *See the silver lining.* If the market drops, that'll hurt the value of your existing investments. But if you are regularly adding fresh savings to your portfolio, you're also benefiting from the decline, because your next investment will buy shares at cheaper prices. Indeed, if you're in your twenties or thirties, the current value of your portfolio is probably modest compared to the dollars you'll invest in the decades ahead.

❖ *Focus on all your assets.* Even if a market decline knocks 20% or 30% off the value of your stock portfolio, it's unlikely your total wealth has declined that much. After all, you might have money in bonds and bank accounts, a home that you own, your future Social Security benefit, any pension you're entitled to, and – maybe most important – your human capital, all of which remain as valuable as ever.

❖ *Remember that stocks have fundamental value.* At times of market turmoil, shares can seem like little more than numbers on an account statement, and those numbers keep shrinking. But behind those declining stock prices are real businesses, which produce goods and services that folks buy every day. Eventually, investors will recognize the value that's there, and they'll bid share prices back up.

Financial wisdom is the realization that our first reaction often needs to be second-guessed.

Day Sixty Seven

Keeping Your Balance

T he goal of investing is to buy low and sell high. This sounds easy, but it isn't. We get swept up in the euphoria of rising markets and invest more in stocks than we should. We're spooked by plunging markets – and find ourselves paralyzed and perhaps even panicking and selling.

How can you avoid this foolishness? It all starts with your asset allocation. You set target percentages for your basic mix of stocks and bonds, and also for cash investments and alternative investments if you plan to include those in your portfolio. For instance, your target allocation might be 55% stocks, 35% bonds, 5% alternative investments, and 5% cash investments. Every so often, you should check where your portfolio stands relative to those target percentages.

If you have more than the 55% you intended for stocks – which will happen when a market rally increases the value of your stock holdings – you should do a little selling to get your stock allocation back in line with your target. Conversely, during a market decline, you'll find yourself with less in stocks than planned. That should prompt you to shift some money from other parts of your portfolio so you get your stocks back up to 55%.

This process of occasionally tweaking your investment mix is known as *rebalancing*. It's a great discipline to adopt, and it'll force you to buy low and sell high. Along the way, you'll control how much risk you're taking, as you keep your stock allocation at a level that makes you comfortable and makes sense given your time horizon.

If all you own are target-date retirement funds, you won't have to worry about rebalancing, because the funds will do it for you. But everybody else should probably look to rebalance at least once a year – and perhaps sooner if a big market move throws your portfolio badly out of whack.

Today's homework: Settle on a date each year to rebalance your portfolio. Many folks do it right at the end of the year, but any date is fine, just so long as you stick with it.

❑ Every year, I will rebalance my portfolio on ⬭⬭⬭⬭⬭⬭⬭⬭ (insert date).

> The moment we think we know which direction the financial markets are headed, we have lost our way.

Day Sixty Eight

Negative Bonds

Whoen we think about our money, we tend to engage in so-called mental accounting, viewing our paycheck, portfolio, house, car, and insurance policies as separate financial buckets. But in fact, all these different financial buckets are related to one another, and we make smarter choices when we see the connections between them. One connecting thread: Many parts of our financial lives look like bonds.

A bond is an investment that pays us regular income. But we can potentially get regular income from many other sources – not just bonds but also from our employer, certificates of deposit, savings accounts, Social Security, and any pension and income annuities we have. We should factor this into our portfolio's design.

For instance, during our working years, we have less need to own bonds – because we have a paycheck to provide us with regular income – and instead, we can take the risk of keeping our portfolio mostly in stocks. Similarly, if much of our retirement expenses will be covered by Social Security and a traditional pension plan, we might allocate less to bonds and continue to hold a stock-heavy portfolio, even after we quit the workforce.

That brings us to a simple but powerful idea: In addition to all these bond lookalikes, we may have a large position in "negative bonds," thanks to our mortgage, student loans, credit card balances, car loans, and other debts. While bonds pay us interest, these debts charge us interest – and the interest we're charged is typically higher than the yield on our bonds.

Let's say we have $200,000 in bonds and $200,000 in debt. Arguably, our net bond position is zero. This has two key implications. First, our overall finances may be riskier than we imagine. Second, instead of buying more bonds, we might want to pay down debt. It could even make sense to sell our bonds and use the proceeds to pay back the money we owe.

> Paying down debt offers a guaranteed return – one that typically outpaces bonds. No investment can make that claim.

Day Sixty Nine

Borrowed Time

Debt isn't necessarily bad. Without it, many of us could never pay for college, buy our first car, or purchase a house. But while debt can help us launch our financial lives, we should be careful not to take on more debt than we can comfortably handle – and we may want to pay off our debts faster than the lender requires.

This is clearly the case with credit card debt, which can charge an outrageous interest rate. But what about other debts? On day 44, you calculated your net worth, which included listing all the debts you have. Below, list those debts again – but this time add the interest rate you're paying:

Debt	Interest Rate

In a few instances, your true cost may be less than the stated interest rate, because the interest is tax-deductible. That can be the case with mortgages, student loans and the interest charged on a margin account at a brokerage firm. You can deduct your mortgage and margin interest if you itemize your deductions on your federal tax return, rather than taking the standard deduction. Meanwhile, you can deduct your student loan interest as long as your income isn't too high.

If any of this interest is deductible – and that's a big if – you might save 12 or 22 cents in taxes for every $1 you pay in interest. The precise amount will depend on your marginal income tax bracket. But the result is that, if the interest rate on your mortgage is 4%, your actual cost might be closer to 3%.

That might sound like a sweet deal. But think about the bonds and bond funds you can buy. There's a good chance they pay less interest than your mortgage is costing you, even after taking any tax savings into account. Moreover, if you owned these bonds and bond funds in a regular taxable account, you'd likely have to pay taxes on the interest you earn, so you would pocket even less.

The bottom line: It often makes sense to pay down debt. Consider the investment opportunities available to you. You'll want to make it your top priority to contribute to your 401(k) plan, especially if there's a matching employer contribution. Next, you should pay down any credit card debt. Next, fund an IRA.

Done all that? If your next step is to invest in stock index funds in your regular taxable account, that's probably a smart move. But if you're inclined to leave any extra savings in the bank or use it to buy bonds, you should probably pay down debt instead, even if it's low-cost mortgage debt.

What if your mortgage seems particularly costly? If the balance outstanding is $100,000 or more and you don't plan to move within the next three years, look into refinancing. That involves taking out a new mortgage with a rate that's usually at least one percentage point lower. Make sure the length of the new loan is no greater than the time left on your existing loan. For instance, if your current loan has 22 years until it will be paid off, refinance it with a 22-year loan or shorter.

Got changes in mind for your debts? List the steps you plan to take:

If we want to retire in comfort, we should retire our debts first.

Day Seventy

Imposing Order

Suppose you dropped dead tomorrow. I know, it isn't exactly a pleasant thought. Still, at that juncture, all your financial problems would be over. But for your family, they might be just beginning, especially if your affairs are a mess. How difficult would it be to settle your estate and wind down your financial life? To make things easier on your family, maybe you should do a little tidying up now, just in case.

Many of us fall prey to what I call *naïve diversification*. We imagine that we're safer if we use multiple financial advisors, have multiple bank and brokerage accounts, and own multiple funds that invest in the same market sector. But in most cases, this extra safety is an illusion. My advice: Limit yourself to one financial advisor, one bank, and one brokerage firm or mutual fund family, and favor target-date funds and total market index funds that give you exposure to broad market segments. That'll keep your financial life simple.

Also look to limit the financial papers you keep. Hang onto seven years of tax returns and the supporting material, and throw out the rest. If you're brokerage firm or mutual fund company provides cost basis information, there is no reason to keep anything but the latest statement – and even that's likely available online.

In addition, keep only the latest copy of your insurance policies, unless you have an ongoing claim that isn't yet settled or you fear a lawsuit, in which case you should save copies from the affected years, plus any other relevant documents. If you're a homeowner, keep all records that detail home improvements. If you ever sell, you'll need those to calculate your home's cost basis. Finally, draw up a consolidated list of usernames and passwords, and put it somewhere safe – but make sure trusted family members know where to find it.

❑ Yes, my financial affairs are well organized.

> Our only earthly immortality will be the recollection of others. Make sure those memories are good.

Day Seventy One

Playing Favorites

Are there charities, political groups, or religious institutions you would like to support? Which organizations or individuals do you want to inherit your money? Make a list of who you wish to help financially, how much help you'd like to provide, and whether you want to give away this money during your lifetime or upon your death.

Who	How Much	When

Give and we will receive: Spending on others often delivers greater happiness than spending on ourselves.

Day Seventy Two

Moving On

Estate planning sounds complicated – and it can be if you're super-wealthy, you own homes in more than one state, you have a family member with special needs, or you have been married more than once and you have both a current spouse and children from earlier marriages whom you're looking to provide for.

But for most of us, estate planning is straightforward. The goal is to make sure our assets end up with the right people. To that end, we use four strategies:

1. We own property jointly with right of survivorship. When we die, these assets – typically homes and cars – pass automatically to the other owners.

2. We name beneficiaries on our retirement accounts. These accounts should pass directly to the folks we listed.

3. We name beneficiaries on our life insurance. Again, the money involved should pass directly to the folks we named.

4. We draw up a will. This usually governs everything else – the property that's not jointly owned and doesn't have beneficiaries named.

To be sure, there are steps we can take for extra credit, such as establishing powers of attorney, which allow somebody to make health or financial decisions on our behalf, should we become incapacitated. But for most folks still in the workforce, the four strategies above should suffice.

Want to make sure you're in good shape? Go through this checklist:

❑ Yes, I'm happy with the joint ownership arrangements I've established.

❑ Yes, I have the right beneficiaries named on my retirement accounts.

❑ Yes, I have the right beneficiaries listed on my life insurance.

❑ Yes, I have a will.

Finally, here's something you almost certainly don't have to worry about: federal estate taxes. With the individual estate tax exclusion now at more than $11 million, less than 0.1% of deaths each year will result in the payment of federal estate taxes. Instead, for most Americans, the biggest "death tax" is the income tax that will still be owed on the retirement accounts they bequeath. Want to ensure your heirs don't pay that tax? You might explore funding Roth 401(k)s and Roth IRAs, and also converting existing traditional retirement accounts to Roth accounts.

> If you bequeath your stamp collection, your kids will remember you. If you bequeath your Roth IRA, they'll remember you fondly.

Day Seventy Three

Cents and Sensibilities

Arguably, money is the last subject that remains truly taboo. We rarely tell others what we make, how much debt we have, or how much we've amassed in savings – and, if the subject comes up, we'll often shade the truth to make ourselves look better. This is not healthy.

Today's task: Talk to your spouse, children, or parents about either their finances or yours. Amazing things could happen. Maybe you'll get new insight into your spouse's money worries. Perhaps your parents will open up about their finances. Maybe you'll spark your children's interest in investing – and start a dialogue that better prepares them for the adult world. Perhaps most important, you might be motivated to fix your own finances, so these conversations are not an embarrassment but a source of pride.

❏ Yes, I've had an honest conversation about money with my family.

> You could talk to your parents about their retirement finances – or you could skip the awkward conversation and buy a house with a spare bedroom.

Day Seventy Four

Hiring Help

After reading this guide, some readers will feel they have the knowledge and confidence to handle their own finances. But others will want professional help, because their financial situation is complicated or because they struggle to save diligently and invest intelligently. What should you look for in an advisor? Here are five pieces of advice:

1. Don't use an insurance agent as your principal financial advisor. An insurance agent will sell you costly insurance products, like variable annuities and cash-value life insurance, that typically prove to be mediocre investments.

2. Don't use a broker who works on commission. In many situations, brokers aren't legally required to act in your best interest – and they have a financial incentive to get you to make unnecessary trades and to sell you products that charge the highest commissions.

3. Consider a robo-advisor if you have a fairly simple financial life. Robo-advisors, such as Betterment, FutureAdvisor, and Rebalance IRA, typically charge low fees and invest clients' money in low-cost index funds. Also check out the low-cost advisory services offered by major financial firms, such as Charles Schwab's Intelligent Portfolios and Vanguard Group's Personal Advisor Services.

4. Look for a fee-only financial planner if you have more than $250,000 in savings and your finances are complicated. While most robo-advisors are focused almost exclusively on portfolio management, a good financial planner will assist with other areas of your financial life, including insurance, estate planning, and taxes.

5. Consider paying by the hour. Relatively few financial advisors charge by the hour, and that hourly fee can seem steep. Still, it could prove cheaper than hiring a financial planner who might charge an annual fee equal to 1% of your portfolio's value. Keep in mind that you'll be responsible for buying the

investments that an hourly advisor suggests. Not sure you'll follow through on an hourly advisor's recommendations? You might want to use a robo-advisor or a fee-only planner.

The virtues of cash-value life insurance are self-evident — to the salespeople who collect huge commissions selling it.

Day Seventy Five

The Virtuous Cycle

W hen you take those first steps toward a better financial life, progress can seem agonizingly slow. It takes time to pay down debt and build up savings. But if you keep plugging away, you will find yourself in a virtuous financial cycle that feeds on itself – and propels you to astonishing riches. That virtuous cycle has three elements.

First, as you step up your savings rate and start to accumulate some wealth, you should be able to cut your living costs, which then allows you to save even more. Where do those cost savings come from? As you build up your bank and financial accounts, you're less likely to incur fees for overdrawing your account or having balances below the required minimum. As you whittle down your debts, you'll pay less in interest each month – and you may reach the point where you never need to borrow, even for large purchases like cars and homes.

As your savings grow, you might also be comfortable raising the deductibles on your health, homeowner's and auto insurance, and lengthening the elimination periods on your disability and long-term-care insurance. That'll trim your premium payments and give you yet more money to save. You might even decide you can drop some policies entirely.

Second, if you buy a house, you'll lock in your housing costs at current prices. True, your property taxes, maintenance expenses, and homeowner's insurance premiums might rise over time. But if you take out a fixed-rate mortgage, your monthly principal-and-interest payments will be fixed, which means they'll become more affordable as your income rises, even if those income increases are simply because of inflation. That'll leave you with even more money to save.

Third, if you regularly sock away 12% to 15% of your income for retirement, your portfolio should hit a tipping point after a dozen or 15 years. What's the tipping point? Each year's investment gains will start to rival and eventually surpass the amount you're actually saving. Thanks to that combination of healthy investment performance and regular savings, your portfolio will be firing on both cylinders, and it could start growing by leaps and bounds.

But to enjoy the benefits of the virtuous cycle, you need to get started – and the sooner, the better.

> It's almost impossible to get rich overnight, but surprisingly easy to get rich over time.

Day Seventy Six

What Money Buys

How can we use money to make our lives better? Obviously, money allows us to buy goods and services, both today and in the future. But much of the time, we end up running in place: We get a brief thrill from our latest purchase, only to find our happiness falls back to where it was. We have a moment of relief when we pay the latest crop of bills, only to find there's a new batch to deal with. We manage to save some money, only to wish our account balances were even larger.

How can we get off this treadmill and get more happiness from our money? I would focus on three broad areas.

First, we should strive to put our financial worries behind us. I think money is sort of like health. It's only when we're sick that we realize how great it is to feel healthy. Similarly, it's only when we're broke that we realize how great it feels to be in good financial shape. In short, we want to get to the point where money isn't a regular source of anxiety. That'll mean something different for each of us. But we might find that financial peace of mind lies in a fat emergency fund, no credit card debt, and the knowledge that we're regularly saving toward retirement and other long-term goals.

Second, we should design a life for ourselves where we can spend our days doing what we love. Relaxing can be enjoyable. But for most of us, the real pleasure lies in work – as long as it is work we think is important, we find challenging, we are passionate about, and we feel we're good at. Think about those moments of flow during the week, when you are totally absorbed in what you're doing and time just whizzes by. Try to rejigger your home and work life – and how you use your money – so you have more of these moments of flow.

Finally, we get great pleasure from spending time with friends and family. Again, you might rejigger your schedule – and how you use your money – so you can spend more time with those you care about. That could mean arranging special family dinners, organizing outings with friends, and making it a point to go out regularly with colleagues at lunchtime.

> A fatter bank account won't necessarily make us happier, but an empty one will likely make us miserable.

Day Seventy Seven

Final Wishes

magine you were writing your own obituary or you were helping a family member prepare the eulogy that'll be delivered after your death. Think about the things you have done that you are especially proud of – perhaps career successes, help you've provided to your family, or ways you have contributed to the larger community. List some of those accomplishments:

_____

_____

_____

_____

_____

_____

_____

_____

_____

_____

_____

_____

_____

What further accomplishments would you like to add to that list? If you could achieve three or five significant things during the rest of your life, what would they be?

It isn't too late. If you seize control of your financial life, you'll buy yourself freedom for the years ahead, and you could use that freedom to accomplish astonishing things. Sound exciting? What are you waiting for?

> If you spend your days doing what you love and your evenings with those you love, you have a rich life – even if you aren't rich.

Acknowledgments

This is not the book I originally planned to write. Rather, I had been wrestling with three different projects: a series of pithy financial insights, a collection of questions designed to probe readers' financial views, and a step-by-step guide that would help someone get his or her finances in shape. None seemed to quite work on its own. But one day, it dawned on my befuddled brain that together, they might work very nicely. I hope you agree.

For the past four years, John Wiley & Sons editor Bill Falloon and I have kicked around various book ideas, failing each time to reach an agreement. It took far too long, but I'm glad we finally made it to the altar.

My agent on this book was the beautiful, sweet, caring Lucinda Karter of the Jennifer Lyons Agency. Inappropriate comment? Fear not: Lucinda's my wife.

Finally, this book is dedicated to the three Js – June, Joan, and Jerry – my mother, mother-in-law, and father-in-law. Each is a rock in his or her own way, always armed with a ready smile, a knowing look, an easy laugh, and a generosity of spirit. At a time when I'm supposed to play the adult for others, I couldn't ask for three better role models.

About the Author

Jonathan Clements is the founder of HumbleDollar.com and author of seven earlier personal finance books, including *How to Think about Money*. He sits on the advisory board and investment committee of Creative Planning, one of the country's largest independent financial advisors.

Jonathan spent almost 20 years at *The Wall Street Journal*, most of that time as the newspaper's personal finance columnist. He also worked for six years at Citigroup, where he was director of financial education for Citi Personal Wealth Management. An avid bicyclist and occasional runner, Jonathan was born in London, England, and graduated from Cambridge University. He's married, with two children and two stepchildren, and lives just north of New York City.

If you want to read more of Jonathan's writing, head to Humble-Dollar.com. There, you can check out his latest blogs, sign up for his free monthly newsletter, and dig into HumbleDollar's comprehensive money guide, which offers additional details on many of the financial issues discussed in this book.